Ancient Scripts in South America

CLYDE WINTERS

Copyright © 2015 Clyde Winters

All rights reserved.

DEDICATION

To people who love truth.

CONTENTS

	Introduction	1
1	Sumer-Akkad	21
2	Sumerians in South America	40
3	The Decipherment of the Fuente Magna Bowl	45
4	The Pokotia Monument	67
5	Inca Writing	103
6	The Axumites in South America	123
7	NSACA	150
8	The Malians in South America	158
9	Final Word	173

ACKNOWLEDGMENTS

I WOULD LIKE TO THANK WILLIAM JAMES VEALL FOR THE DATA ON THE MALIAN INSCRIPTIONS FROM URUGUAY

Introduction

Pedro Ciezo de Leon in 1553 wrote that "In this new world of the Indies, as they knew nothing of letters, we are in a state of blindness concerning many things"[1].

There are many mysteries about ancient

Bolivia/Peru. One of these mysteries is Tihuanaca.

Although many people are aware of the ancient city

---

[1] Hugh Thompson, <u>The White Rock: an exploration of the Inca heartland</u> (New York: The Overlook Press, 2001), p.xviv.

of Tihuanaca, they don't know about the many mysterious artifacts relating to ancient South America found in the museums of many South American cities.

In 2000, a group of South American archaeologists , belonging to Unidad de Arqueologia y Antropologia de Bolivia or UNAAR, Bernardo Biados, Freddy Arce, Javier Escalente, Cesar Calisaya, Leeocadio Ticlla, Alberto Vasquez, Alvaro Ferholz, Omar Sadud, Paulo Batuani and Rodrigo Velasco began a search of Bolivian museums which will change the history of writing in South America. The discoveries by this team of Bolivian archaeologists was supported by the Honorable H. Enrique Toro, past President of the Congress of Bolivia. Led by Bernardo Biados, these archaeologists began to search South American museums to determine if South Americans had writing prior to Christopher Columbus' discovery of America.

Alexander von Humboldt, in <u>Vues des cordillieres et monuments des peuples indigenes de Amerique</u> (1824) wrote that "It has been recently not in doubt that the Peruvians had besides Quippus , knowledge of a sign script".

Archaeologists have long recognized that the Inca had a system to record information called quipus. The quipu system was a communication system that used knots on cords to record Incan official records.

Considerable ink has been used to write about the absence of a formal writing system among the Inca.

The only system of writing believed to have existed among the Inca was quipu.

Quipu was a system of knots strategically placed on a cord, to record knowledge. This system of knotted record keeping was originally introduced to the Inca by the Huari [2]. The records were read by the **quipucamayos**, men skilled in interpreting the quipu.

The search of museums by Biados and UNAAR led to startling discoveries. In these museums the archaeologists found an engraved bowl from Fuente Magna, with symbols identical to Sumerian cuneiform and Proto-Sumerian syllabic symbols. This discovery of Fuente Magna provided startling testimony to the possible use of writing in Bolivia thousands of years

---

[2] Ibid., p.247.

before the Spanish reached the New World in 1492. Because the writing was in a known language, Dr. Clyde Winters was able to decipher the writing on the bowl. This decipherment provides us with keen insight into the culture of the ancient Bolivians and suggested that some ancient Bolivians may have come from Sumer an ancient civilization that formerly existed in Mesopotamia.

Another mystery is the Putaki statue from Pokotia, Bolivia. The Putaki statue is a true mystery, because it helps us see the ancient and wonderful presence of ancient writing in South America. The Pokotia statue was found at a site 15 km from Tihuanaca.

The Pokotia monolith is interesting because it resembles many statues found at Tihuanaca. Examination of the Pokotia statue by the Research team indicated that the statue had writing on it. This was a significant find by the team. Evidence of writing on the Pokotia monolith suggested that the ancient Bolivians had their own writing in ancient times.

In an attempt to find out what was written on the legs of the Pokotia statue, Bernardo sent the inscriptions to epigraphers around the world via the World Wide Web. Dr. Winters, recognized that the signs on the Pokotia monolith and Fuente magna bowl were identical, and indicated that the writing on the statue might be readable using the Sumerian language to interpret the meaning of the writing on the Pokotia statue.

This new inscribed statue from Bolivia, is important for two reasons. First, it confirmed Biados', hypothesis that the South Americans had writing in ancient times.

Secondly, the Pokotia statue was important because it possessed signs similar to the symbols on the Fuente Magna bowl. The appearance of identical signs on the Fuente Magna bowl and the Pokotia monolith, supported the view that continuity existed between the writing on these monuments.

The Pokotia statue also made it clear that literacy existed among the South Americans for millennia, eventhough many scholars believed the South Americans were illiterate until the Spanish conquered the Inca of Bolivia-Peru. For example, Sally Jane Wolfe Gordon, in her dissertation wrote that "although universities and writing systems are attributed to a pre-Incan era, such must be assumed to be mythological"[3].

It is interesting to note that Sitchin published a picture of skin parchment he claims was formerly in the Peruvian museum at La Paz Bolivia, that have many of the signs found on the Fuente Magna bowl and the Proto-Sumerian script[4]. According to Sitchin, it was published by Ribero and von Tschudi, in Reisen durch Sudamerika. This parchment may still exist in a Bolivian museums[5].

---

[3] Sally J. Wolfe Gordon, The Inca Empire: A test case for a hypothesis on schooling in civilizational states (Unpublished Ph.D. dissertation, University of Illinois at Urbana-Champagne, 1978), p.151.
[4] Zecharia Sitchin, The Lost Realms (N.Y.: Avon Books, 1990), p.150.
[5] In a personal communication to the author Nernardo Biados, told me that he has personally seen these skin parchments that contain writing.

Ancient Scripts in South America

The idea that the Inca and earlier peoples of Bolivia-Peru had writing and centers of learning, is not new[6]. Incan traditions make it clear that they had long possessed both writing and learning centers, centuries before the Spanish settled the area[7]. Our knowledge about Inca writing comes from the historian Fernando Montesinos, who visited Peru from 1629-1642. Montesinos traveled around Peru for fifteen years collecting material for his work <u>Memorias Antiguas Historiales del Peru</u> [8]. He recorded many Incan traditions that acknowledged

---

[6] Roberto MacLean y Estenos<u>, Sociologica educacional en el abtiguo Peru </u>. Mexico: Biblioteca de ensayos sociologicos instituto de investigaciones socials universidad nacional , 1955.
[7] David H. Childress (Ed.), <u>Far Out Adventures</u>, Kempton, Ill.: Adventures Unlimited Press, 2001.
[8] . Fernando Montesinos, <u>Memorias antiguas historialas del Peru</u>, trans. By Phillip Ainsworth. London: Hakluyt Society, 1920.

the presence of writing and educational institutions among the Inca[9]. In regards to Andean education, Montesinos wrote that:

> "He [Torca Apu Capac, the fortieth king of ancient Peru] founded in Cuzco a Univeristy , which was celebrated among them because of their small learning. And in time, according to what the Indians say, there were letters and characters upon parchment and on the leaves of trees, until all this was lost for a period of four hundred years"[10].

Although the Spanish observers called the Incan centers of learning universities, Roberto MacLean y Estenos noted that " nothing gives us the authority to talk about the existence of a university in the Incan

---

[9] Steven J. Crum, College before Columbus: Mayans, Aztecs and Incas offered advanced education long before the arrival of Europeans. <u>Tribal College Journal of American Indian Higher Education</u> , 7 (2), (10/31/1991) pp.14-25; and John Collier, <u>The Indians of the Americas</u> (New York,W.W. Norton and Company, Inc., 1947), p.56.
[10] Montesinos, p.53.

Ancient Scripts in South America

Empire, although there did exist centers of a select culture (education) destined to the imperial aristocracy. They were called the Yachuhuasi"[11]. I disagree, if the Spanish observers of these institutions called them universities, the Yachahuasi, were in fact universities, no matter what modern writers might say.

The Incan colleges existed up to the time Hernando Pizarro entered Cuzco. The historian Germán Arcineigas wrote that in 1533, Pizarro saw "the monumental Quechua [Incan] university "[12].

This university may be the Yachahuasi, which was used to train noblemen and administrators for the

---

[11] MacLean y Estenos, p.80.
[12] Germán Arciniegas, Latin America: A cultural history, trans. By Joan MacLean (New York; Alfred A. Knopf, 1967), p.9.

Incan state. This University was founded by Sinchi or Cinche Roca at Cuzco[13]. The university was expanded by the ninth Incan king, Pachacutec[14]. Antonio Vazquez de Espinosa, a chronicler of the 1620's, noted that:

" To clearly follow with the description of this city of Incas (cuzco) we have to come back to the Huacapunca neighborhood, also called the sanctuary's door, that was located north of the central part of the city. On the south side of that park there was a university founded by king Inca Roca.That university was actually a group of school buildings called the 'schools' neighborhood and known as Yacha Huaci. This was the home of wisemen known as Amautas and poets that would teach science to the students "[15]

---

[13] Collier, p.56.
[14] Ibid., p.56.
[15] Daniel Valcarcel, Historia de la educacion incaica (Lima: Editorial Lima, 1960), p. 113.

Ancient Scripts in South America

The Chronicler Montesinos mentions the tradition of writing among the Inca. This writing was probably taught at the Incan Yachahuaci along with quipus.

D.H. Childress quoting from Hiram Bingham's monumental history of his discovery of Machu Pichu in 1911, titled the <u>Lost City of the Incas,</u> provides an interesting account of writing among the Incas by Montesinos. Commenting on the rule of Pachacuti VII, Montesinos wrote that "As the people obeyed him with so little certainty, and as they were so greatly corrupted in the matter of religion and customs, he took steps to conquer them, because he said that if those people communicated with his, they would corrupt them with the great vices to which they had given temselves up like ungovernable beasts. Therefore, he tactfully sent messengers in all directions, asking the chiefs to put a stop to superstition and to the adoration of many gods and animals which they adored; and the outcome of this was but a slight mending of their ways and the slaying of the ambassadors. The king dissembled for the time being and made great sacrifices and appeals to **Illatici Huira Cocha**. One reply was that the cause of the pestilence had been letters and that no one ought to use them nor resuscitate them for, from their employment great harm would come. Therefore Tupac Cauri commanded by law, that under the pain of death, no one should traffic in **quilcas,** which were the parchments and leaves of trees on which they used to write, nor should there be any use of letters. They observed this oracular command with so much care that after this loss the Peruvians never

Ancient Scripts in South America

used letters and because in later times a learned ***amautu*** invented some characters, they burnt him alive , and from this time forth, they used threads and quipus"[16].

This tradition said that the Inca were not allowed to use writing by Pachacuti very interesting. It is interesting because many ancient Incan ***mantas*** or weavings show characters identical to the writing found on the Fuente Magna and Pokotia statute. Many of these ***manta*** with writing were published by Felipe Guaman Poma de Ayala's <u>Nueva coronica y buen gobierno</u> of Peru. The <u>Nueva coronica y buen gobierno</u> provides many interesting facts about the governance, cultural history and religion of the Inca.

---

[16] Childress, p.438.

It has many drawings of Incan dignitaries whose clothing show numerous symbols that relate to the writing found on Fuente Magna and the Pokotia monolith. The letters on the mantas can be read using Sumerian.

There is an Incan tradition that manta were used to record history. Hugh Thompson, in <u>The White Rock: An exploration of the Inca heartland</u>, discussed the textile that recorded the "history of Tupac Amaru", the last Emperor of the Incas[17].Thompson called these textiles "oral histories" of the Incas[18]. Thompson wrote that: "It is these weavings that much of the oral history of the Andes has found its promptings, along with the quipus, the knotted cords.

---

[17] Thompson, p.274.
[18] Ibid., p.275

This was perhaps one reason why cloth was so obsessively valued by the Incas, far more than if it were just for clothing. There are numerous stories of retreating Inca armies burning the cloth in their warehouses...."[19]. Thompson continued "the Spanish never understood the secret messages contained within the mantas, the weavings, just as they never understood the system of the quipus"[20].

The fact that the Spanish never noticed that the Inca used the mantas to record history, may explain why up to now no one noticed that the mantas, also include writing that relate to writing on the Fuente Magna Bowl and Pokotia statue by Bolivian archaeologists.

---

[19] Ibid., p.274.
[20] Ibid., p.277.

William Burns Glynn, in La escritura de los Incas, identified ten symbols on the Incan mantas, that he regards as writing[21]. These symbols collected by Glynn are identical to signs found on the Fuente Magna and Pokotia statue. These symbols are also analogous to the Proto-Sumerian writing of the people of ancient Sumer

A.H Verrill and R. Verrill [22], and J. Bailey in Sailing to Paradise [23], maintain that the area around Lake Titicaca may have been called Lake Manu, by the Sumerian. Bernardo Biados's discovery of the Pokotia monument supports the research of the Verrills that

---

[21] William B.Glynn, La escritura de los incas. Lima ,Peru: Editorial Los Pinos, 1981.
[22] A.H Verrill and R. Verrill, Americas ancient civilizations . New York: Putnam, 1953.
[23] J. Bailey Sailing to Paradise. New York: Simon & Schuster, 1994.

the Sumerians came to South America in search of metals.

The Sumerians called their nation and themselves ***Ki en gi*** "land of the true lords", the name Sumer , comes from the Assyrians who called these people ***sumir-itu*** "the sacred language".

In upcoming pages we will discuss the Sumerian writing from Fuente Magna and Pokotia. We will also discuss the evidence of Semitic writing found in South America that indicates that in addition to Sumerians, Semitic speaking people also made their way to South America in ancient times.

In summary , the South Americans probably had there own writing system The fact that the writing appears to be analogous to writing used by the Sumerians, and the identification of Sumerian placenames in on the Altiplano leads us to believe that Bolivia and Peru, may represent the "Tin Land of the West" mentioned in the Sumerian inscriptions. If this is true ancient Bolivia-Peru may have been called the "Sunset Land", by the ancient Sumerians.

CHAPTER 1: SUMER-AKKAD

Around 4000 to 3500 BC a group of people entered Mesopotamia from the east who founded the civilization of Sumer. These people called themselves "black-heads".

The Sumerians and Elamites came to Mesopotamia by Boats first used in the Eastern Sahara and on the Red Sea are analogous to Sumerian craft.

The Sumerian, Dravidian and African speakers originated in the Fertile African Crescent, which were the Highland regions of Middle Africa. These people belonged to the Maa Clan. The Maa Confederation was the name of the major Paleo-African clan during the last great wet period in Saharan history 5000-3000 B.C. The Maa confederation includes the Egyptians, Elamites, Dravidians, Manding and Sumerians. In this paper we call members of this civilization: Proto-Saharans. To denote their ethnic origin they added the term **Ma,** to their ethnonyms, e.g., the Manding called themselves **Ma-nde** (the children of **Ma**); and the

Sumerians called themselves **Mah-Gar-ri** (exalted God's children)[24].

The Sumerians were in control of Mesopotamia for many years. Then around 2334 BC, a group of Puntite Speakers called Akkadians under Naram-Sin or Sargon of Agade took over Mesopotamia.

The most famous king of Sumer was Gilgamesh. The first king to unify much of Sumer though was Mesilim, who took the title of King of Kish around 2500 BC.

The second famous leader was Gudea. Gudea is best known for his trade expeditions and unification of Sumer. He is also said to have obtained craftsmen from Susa and Elam for the decoration of temples for his people.

By 2380 BC the Semitic people took control of Sumer. The Semitic-speakers were led by Sargon the Great. It was Sargon who unified all of Sumer.

Sargon who had once been the cup bearer of the King of Ur-Zababa a king of Kish. He was also a

---

[24] Clyde A. Winters, The Proto-Culture of the Dravidians, Manding and Sumerians, Tamil Civilization,3(1), 1-9.

great military leader and builder of the unified state of Sumer-Akkad. The capital of his empire was Agade", Akkad of the Bible.

By 2000 BC, the Akkadians had been subjugated by the Shubartu, a people with Indo-European names. Also at this time Amorites entered Mesopotamia . Part of this invasion were the Canaanites who also spoke a Semitic language. The Canaanites established the rule of Hammurabi in 1800 or 1700 BC.

The fact that the Sumerians and Akkadians were Africoid or Black is best indicated by the art works from Ur, Tell Asmar, and Eridu.

Indo-European rulers of Lagash and Larsa tried to imitate Sumerian styles, but many of them were Gutians and therefore not of Kushite origin. It is interesting to note that the Mesopotamia King-List, does not recognize many of the "ensi" of Lagash. The Gutians, ruled Lagash until Uthuhegal King of Erech conquered Tirigan the last Gutian King.

The Canaanites invaded Mesopotamia from Arabia, they occupied Palestine and Phoenicia. In the ancient literature the Canaanites were called "Martu" or Amorites. The most famous Canaanite ruler of Mesopotamia was Hammurabi.

Hammurabi was a great Black King. He is famous for collecting the lawsof Babylon and creating a code to give justice to all Babylonians.

Another group of Canaanites, the Kassites became the rulers of Mesopotamia. The Kassites ruled for 400 years, far longer than any other Babylonian dynasty. They were very good rulers of Babylonia.

The Kassites maintained good relations with the Egyptians. This fact is supported by the Amarna cuneiform inscriptions found at the capital of Pharoah Akhenaten.

Sumerian Connections

There is unity between the Akkadian and Ethiopian languages. The Akkadians and Sumerians claim they came from the Egypto-Nubia and Punt (Ethiopia) to west Asia.

Rawlinson was convinced that there was a relationship between the Sumerians and Africans. As a result he used two African languages: one Semitic and the other Cushitic to decipher the cuneiform writing.

Rawlinson was sure that the ancient Nubians and Puntites founded Mesopotamian civilization [25].

---

[25] C.B. Rawlinson, "Notes on the early history of Babylon", Jour. Royal Asiatic Society (First Series) 15, p.230.

The Sumerians may have come from the Sahara before it became a desert. Affinities exist between Nubia ware and pottery from Ennedi and Tibesti.

These Saharan people were round-headed ancient Mediterranean type. They were often referred to as Cafsa or Capsians; a group of people not devoid of Negroid characteristics according to J Desanges[26]. Wyatt MacGaffey, claims that the term "Mediterranean" is an anthropological euphemism for "Negro".

The boats of the Saharan people are similar to those found on ancient engravings of boats in Mesopotamia and the Indus Valley. Many of the boats found in the eastern desert of Egypt and among the Red Sea Hills show affinities to Mesopotamian models.

S.N. Kramer in The Sumerians, claimed that Makan was Egypt, Mekluhha was Nubia-Punt, and the Indus Valley was Dilmun. Today Dilmun is believed to be found near Arabia. But the archaeological evidence suggest that the Indus Valley

---

[26] J. Desanges, "The Proto-Berbers". In General History of Africa vol.2, (Ed.) by G. Mokhtar (Heinemann Educational Books, London) p.25.

which was settled by Dravidian speakers was the source of the lapis lazuli, which made Dilmun famous [27].

Archaeological research has confirmed that cultural interaction existed between the contemporary civilizations of the 4th and 3rd millennia B.C.

Extensive trade routes connected the Proto-Dravidians of the Indus Valley, with African people in Egypto-Nubia, and the Elamites and Sumerians. P. Kohl discovered that vessels from IVBI workshop at Tepe Yahya, have a uniform shape and design. Vessels sharin

g this style are distributed from Soviet Uzbekistan to the Indus Valley, and Sumerian, Elamite and Egyptian sites [28]. In addition, we find common arrowheads at Harappan sites, and sites in Iran, Egypt, Minoan Crete and Heladic Greece.

It appears that the locus for this distribution of cultural traditions and technology was the Saharan-Nubian zone or Kush. This would explain why the Sumerians and Elamites often referred to themselves

---

[27] Philip L. Kohl, "The balance of trade in the mid-Third millennium BC", Current Anthropology, 19 (1978), pp.463-492.

[28] Ibid, p.466.

as "ksh". For example the ancient Sumerians called their dynasty "Kish". The words "kish", "kesh" and "kush" were also names for ancient Nubia-Sudan.

The Elamites also came from Kush. According to the classical writer Strabo, Susa the centre of the Elamite civilization was founded by Tithonus, king of Kush.

B.B. Lal has shown conclusively that the Dravidians came from Nubia and were related to the C-Group people who founded the Kerma dynasty [29].

They both used a common black-and-red ware (BRW) which Lal found was analogous to ceramics used by the megalithic people in India who also used analogous pottery signs identical to those found in the corpus of Indus Valley writing [30].

Singh believes that this pottery spread from Nubia, through Mesopotamia and Iran southward into India

---

[29] B.B. Lal, "From megalithic to the Harappan: Tracing back the graffiti on pottery", Ancient India, 16 (1960).
[30] B.B. Lal, "The only Asian mission in threatened Nubia", The Illustrated London Times>, 20 April 1963.

[31]. The earliest examples of this BRW date to the Amratian period (c4000-3500 B.C.).

This same BRW was found at the lowest levels of Harappan sites at Lothal and Rangpur. After 1700 B.C. This ceramic tradition spread southward into megalithic India [32].

Dilmun was an important source of lapis lazuli. If the Indus Valley civilization was Dilmun as hypothesized by Kramer, it would explain the control of the Harappans/ or Dilmunites of this important metal.

The Indus Valley people spoke a Dravidian language[33]. The Harappans controlled the lazurite region of Badakhshan, and the routes to the tin and copper fields of central Asia[34].

---

[31] H.N. Singh, History and Archaeology of Black-and-Red Ware, Delhi, 1982.

[32] C.A. Winters, The Dravido-Harappan Colonization of Central Asia, Central Asiatic Journal, 34 (1-2), pp.120-144.

[33] C.A. Winters, "The Dravidian language of the Harappan script",Archiv Orientalni, (1990).

[34]) B. Brenjes, "On Proto-Elamite Iran", Current anthropology, 24 (2) (1984), pp. 240-.

The major city of the Harappans/Dilmunites in the lapis lazuli region was Shortughai. Francefort believes that many lapis lazuli works were transported to Iran and Mesopotamia from Shortughai[35]. The BRW at Shortughai is typically Harappan.

Most modern scholar such as Joan Oates, in "<u>Babylon</u>" suggest that Magan (Egypto-Nubia) and "Meluhha" (Punt) were southeastern Arabia and the Makian coast to as far as the Indus Valley. But according to Samuel Noah Krammer, the leading expert on the Sumerians and Akkadians, from the time of Sargon the Great (2334 BC) down to the first millennium BC, "Magan" and "Meluhha" was Egypto-Nubia and Punt (Ethiopia) respectively. According to these records ships from "Meluhha" and "Magan" brought trade goods to Mesopotamia.

According to W.J. Perry, in <u>The Growth of Civilization</u>, the myths, legends and traditions of the Sumerians pointed to Nubia as their ancient home. Sir Henry Rawlinson, who deciphered the cuneiform writing traced the Sumerians and Akkadians back to Nubia and Punt. Sir Rawlinson, called the ancient Mesopotamians "Kushites". It was the French

---

[35] Henri-Paul Franceport, "La civilisation de l'Indus aux rives de l'Oxus", <Archeologie>, (Decembre) p.50.

Orientalist Julius Oppert, who named them Sumerians , in an attempt to keep them separate from the Kushites, a Black race of Africa. But Rawlinson, in the " Journal of the Royal Asiatic , was correct in calling them Kushites.

The title "King of Kish", was highly prized by subsequent Kings of Sumer. This title allowed Sumerian Kings to claim of suzerainty over the whole country.

Dierelafoy, in "L'Acropole de Susa" wrote that "I shall attempt to show to what distant antiquity belongs the establishment of the Negritos upon the left bank of the Tigris and the elements constituting the Susian monarchy ....Towards 2300 BC the plains of the Tigris and Anzan Susinka were ruled by a dynasty of Negro Kings". Herodotus, who visited the area in the 5th century BC mentions the dark skin of this people who he called Ethiopians.

Sir Harry Johnston, noted that the Elamites "appear to have been Negroid people with kinky hair and to have transmitted this racial type to Jews and Syrians".

The people of Sumer, over time learned all their knowledge from the Anu, a mysterious people who founded the Ubaid Culture in Mesopotamia. The Sumerians expanded the dykes to hold back the floods of the Euphrates and Tigris rivers, and dug canals and reservoirs to store water and carry to the plains. This led to grand harvest yielding 200 and 300 grains per plant, in an area today where the Turks make a pitiful existence.

Sumerians built cities of unbaked bricks. Many of these cities such asUr, Erudu and Uruk (Erech), Nippur, Agade (Akkad) have been excavated. The excavations of Erech and Agade support the Biblical accounts and skeletal remains of the ancient inhabitants of Chaldaea, show that they were Blacks. These Southwest Asians were short with thin lips and large noses.

The Sumerians said they came by sea to Sumer-Akkad. Enki, who founded Eridu situated on the head of the Persian Gulf is said to have come by sea.

The Sumerians spoke two different languages one was Semitic, it was used by the Semitic founders of Akkad; and the other language was Sumerian, like the Egyptians said they had come to Mesopotamia from "Magan" or Egypto-Nubia, and "Meluhha" or Punt (northeast Africa). These areas are mentioned as early as Sargon the Great and Gudea. Both countries are frequently in the Sumerian and Akkadian records.

Sargon the Great (2330) wrote that the boats of Magan, Meluhha and Dilmun were anchored in his capital of Agade. Gudea, wrote that he obtained diorite for his statues from Magan and wood for the building of temples from both Magan and Meluhha.

The Meluhhaites were called "the men of the black land" or "the black Meluhhaites". The Meluhhaites are said to have traded in carnelian, lapis lazuli, metals, stones and mineral.

Dilmun, which is believed to be the ancient Indus Valley civilization, was considered to the Paradise by the Sumerians. According to Sumerian traditions Enki, had come from Dilmun. It is interesting to note that Sumerian is closely related to the Dravidian language which was spoken in the Indus Valley in ancient times as pointed out in chapter four.

SUMERIAN SOCIETY

The Sumerian cities were led by an "ensi", who was a city governor. Matters concerning the cities of Sumer were decided on by free-citizens who served in an assembly, consisting of a upper house of elders and lower house of "men".

The King had a regular army with chariots and armored infantry. The Sumerians cherished goodness, truth, law and order and justice. As a result the King had to be a man who could establish law and order and protect the poor from the rich.

The Mesopotamian cities existed only for trade and as centers for worship. As a result the people were heavily taxed, so as to provide income for the temples.

Land could be individually owned in Sumer-Akkad, but most city land was owned by the temple. This land could not be bought or sold.

CALENDAR

The Sumerians invented their own calendar. It was divided into two seasons "**emesh**" and (summer), and "**enten**" (winter). The months were lunar, they began with the evening of the new moon and lasted from 29-30 days in length. The day began with sunset and was 12 double hours in length following the Egyptian model.

MATHEMATICS

The Babylonians had a complex mathematical system. In addition to simple arithmetic these people had algebra. Moreover they employed Pythagorean theorem more than a thousand years before the Greek Pythagoras learned it from the Egyptians. It seems though that Algebra and Geometry were just a few of the mathematical procedures used by the people of Mesopotamia.

ASTROLOGY

The Sumerians were stargazers. The Sumerians called all celestial bodies: planets, stars or constellations MUL, i.e., that which shines in the heights. Some Mul, were called Lu Bad, because they wandered through the heavens. The Sumerians were also familiar with Super Novas.

WRITING

The Sumerians are believed to have invented their own writing system. This writing is called cuneiform, which comes from the Latin word cuneus, this means wedge. The Sumerians wrote their characters on clay with a pen or stylus. Thousands of their tablets have been found at Nippur and Nenevah.

EDUCATION

The Sumerians or Babylonians as the Semitic/Akkadian empire was called had many schools where students learned grammar, writing, medicine and mathematics. The Sumerian schools were called: EDUBBA. Teachers were called ummias or professors.

RELIGION

The Sumerians had many gods, plus a main god called "An", the heaven god. By 2500 BC with the raise of the Akkadians or Babylonians the Supreme god was called Enlil the air-god.

Other Sumerian gods included "Ianna" or the Akkadian goddess "Ishtar" and her husband the Shepard-god Dumuzi the Biblical Tammuz. The Queen of the neither world or hell was called

"Ereshkigal".

The Babylonians had their own names of the gods. The major gods were "Sin" (Nanna) the mood god; "Ishtar", Venus; and "Nabu" or "Marduk" the god of wisdom and knowledge. "Nergal" was the god of war. "Nabu" also the god of the scribes were popularized by them in Babylon,"Nabu" was the son of "Marduk".

Most of the contemporary books on Sumer and ancient Mesopotamia in general, provide little information on the goddesses of Sumer; as a result you would feel that mother-goddess worship was insignificant in Sumer. Although this is the case for contemporary literature, there is considerable discussion of the Sumer goddesses by Samuel N. Kramer, <u>The Sumerians</u>

The most important god in the history of Sumer was Nammu. Nammu was the creator of the heavens and the sea. She was also recognized as the mother of Enki. In Sumerian literature she was recognized as the primeval sea, and "the mother who gave birth to all the gods" [36]. This is an important revelation because it makes it clear that in the beginning the Sumerians held the mother-goddess as the leading god in their pantheon of gods.

---

[36] **Kramer, p.150**

Second important mother goddess in the history of Sumer was Ninhursag. Ninhursag was also called Ninmah ' the exalted lady" and Nintu 'the lady who makes life". In some Sumerian documents Nintu was called Ki "mother earth". Nintu was usually listed as the fourth god in the Sumerian pantheon of gods after An, Enlil and Enki. But Kramer noted that: " in an earlier day this goddess was probably of even higher rank, and her name often preceded that of Enki when the four gods were listed together for one reason or another" [37].

The oldest temple in Sumer was dedicated to Nintu. At al-Ubaid the oldest pottery in Mesopotamia was found. It was also here that the oldest Sumerian temple Enamzu was dedicated to Nintu [38].

The most ancient Sumerian document, is concerned with Adab, a major ancient Sumerian center where Ubaid pottery has been found, was devoted to the building the temple of Enamzu. This temple was dedicated to the chief deity of the city the mother goddess Nintu .

The document, relating to events taking place early in the 3rd millennium B.C., notes that when the temple

---

[37] Ibid., p.122.
[38] Ibid., p.51.

was dedicated the viziers or **sukkalmahs** of Elam, Marhashi, Gutium, Subir, Martu, Sutium and Eanna/Erech, came to bring sacrifices to participate in the celebration at the Adab temple (Kramer, p.50). In relation to this inscription Kramer noted that, "The rather extraordinary dedicatory inscription then closes with the exhortation that the goddess Nintu should grant long life to the ***ensis*** (kings, rulers) of these seven lands if they continue to bring offerings and sacrifices to the Enamzu of Adab" [39]. This document about the dedication of the Enamzu temple is important because it indicates that all of the early Sumerian city-states recognized Nintu, a mother goddess as the premier god of Sumer. This may explain why the early Sumerian rulers described themselves as nourished constantly "by Ninhursag with milk"[40].

The Sumerians made it clear that the goddesses, not the gods, first created life. For example, Nintu according to Kramer was considered to be mother of all living things, and aide to Nammu in the creation of mankind.

In the Sumerian story for the creation of mankind Enki asked his mother to create mankind with the assistance of Ninmah/Nintu. Kramer recorded the

---

[39] Ibid., p.51.
[40] Ibid., p.122.

story as follows: "Oh my mother (Nammu), the creature whose name you uttered, it exists, Bind upon it the image (?) of the gods, mix the heart of the clay that is over the abyss, the god and princely fashioners will thicken the clay, you, do you bring the limbs into existence; Ninmah will work above you, the goddess (of birth)...will stand by you at your fashioning;O my mother, decree its (the new born's) fate, Ninmah will bind upon it the mold (?)of the gods, it is man"[41].

This passage from the Sumerian creation story, makes it clear that mankind was created by the word or decree of Nammu. And a female goddess Nintu created that man in the image of the gods.

The Sumerian literature makes it clear that the male gods were unsuccessful in the creation of life. This is evidenced by the story about the creation of a life form by Enki. In this story, Enki attempts to create a life form, which comes into being sick and lifeless. As a result of Enki's mistake he is cursed by Nintu, and sent to Hades to die[42]

According to the story, the gods find Nintu/Ninhursag and beg her to relieve Enki of her curse. The goddess forgives Enki, and she creates goddess to heal Enki who has been cast into the

---

[41] Ibid., p150.
[42] Ibid., p150.

underworld. This goddess was called Ninti "the lady of the rib" or "the lady who makes life" [43].

This story makes it clear that the male gods of Sumer had almost no role in the creation of mankind. The fact that Nammu is credited with 1) the creation of the heavens and the sea, 2) the protector and legitimizer of the Kings of Sumer, and 3) the god who decreed that man exist; and Nintu, made man in the image of the god, make it clear that the goddess was primeval god of the Sumerians.

Kramer believes that the story in the Bible about the creation of women, from the rib may relate to the story of Ninti. This results from the fact that *ti*, is the Sumerian word for "rib". As a result, the fact that Ninti, was known as the "Lady of the rib" and "the Lady who makes life", may explain why the Bible claims that Eve in the Biblical paradise story was created from the "rib". Kramer believes that since Ninti represented both the making of life and the rib, the writers of the Bible made a "pun" by claiming that Eve was created form the rib, when the Sumerian creation story makes it clear that Ninti, was created by Nintu, to heal Enki.

---

[43] Ibid., p.149.

CHAPTER 2: SUMERIANS IN SOUTH AMERICA

According to the the Verrills and Bailey the Sumerians came to this area in search of tin. They support this view by a discussion of the Sumerian traditions, that Sumerians set sail to the land west of the Mediterranean that they called the **Kuga-Ki** *("Tin land of the West"* or *"the Sunset Land").* The Sumerians in their *Ma-gur* ships could carry 18.5 metric tons of copper.

The Andes, may have been the Tin land or **Kuga-Ki** of the Sumerians. The Andes mountains were originally called *Antis*[44]. This areas was formerly called *Antisuyo*, Kingdom of the Antis. This was also the homeland of the Anti Indians. In the Quechua language spoken by many Indians in the area, *Antis,* means copper and the name for the Indians who

---

[44] J.M. Allen, Atlantis: The Andes solution. New York: St. Martin Press, 1998; and W.H. Prescott, The conquest of Peru. New York: Harper, 1847.

formerly lived in this part of South America.

Antis is probably of non-Quechua origin. The Chipaya language, spoken in the area, is different from Quechua and Aymara. Dr. Swaney, claims that Chipaya is closely related to Arabic and North African tribal languages[45].

This part of Bolivia is famous for the rich minerals found in the area. Many of these metals are found at the Bolivian Altiplano, near Lake Poopo and inland sea , formerly connected to the Pacific Ocean by rivers now dried up.

The Bolivian Altiplano, is the largest plain in the world. It contains two inland seas Lake Titicaca and Lake Poopo[46]. This area high in the Andes mountains make it an apt location for Lake Manu or 'Cloud Lake' of the Sumerians, where metals were mined in the Mountains of Sunset, the land situated west of the Mediterranean Sea.

Lake Poopo is fifty miles long. The lake was surrounded by mountains on all sides and canals. Satellite pictures indicate that deep canals formerly existed near Lake Poopo. It is a shallow sea a few feet deep. Lake Poopo is a salty sea, sometimes known to

---

[45] Deanna Swaney, Bolivia: A travel survival kit. Lonely Planet, 1988.
[46] Allen, p.10.

dry up.

Lake Titicaca and Lake Poopo are connected by the River Desagua *dero*. The companion Lake of Poopo, was Lake Uru. The city of Oruro is located near Lake Uru.

The metals found near Lake Poopo include copper, tin, gold and silver. Here we find metals being extracted in the cities of Oruro and Corocoro where gold and copper were mined. The names for these cities suggest Sumer. In Sumerian the name for city is ***uru***. The suffixes *–oro* for the cities around Lake Poopo, is strikingly similar to ***uru***, the name for city in the Sumerian language.

It is interesting to note that a major center in this area is Potosi. Potosi is famous for its tin deposits.

At Potosi we find the Potosi mountain. The Potosi mountain is made of solid tin and was called Mount Catavi.

The Potosi area was a center of mining. In the 1550's, the Spanish began to exploit the silver found at Potosi Hill.

The Spanish called Potosi Hill, Cerro Rico or "Rich Mountain". As a result of the Spanish attempt to fully exploit the riches in this area " a horrific" number of Indians died in the mines. Thompson vividly describes this tragedy. He says that " the mine consumed the labour-force of Bolivia's Altiplano. If they didn't die, they were ground down by the apology for a wage that was paid to them. Within a generation, the population of those parts of the Altiplano used for mine conscription was haved. Within another generation it had halved again. And still Potosi continued to exact its quota"[47].

In modern history Potosi has been a center for the mining of tin, copper, lead and silver. Located near Tihuanaca, Potosi may have been a center of Sumerian settlement in ancient times like the cities of Oruro and Corocoro. Bailey suggest that Potosi may relate to the Sumerian term Patesi the Sumerian term for 'priest king'.

The metals mined on the Altiplano were transported along the Pilcomyo River or Rio de la Planta today[48]. The Sumerians may have transported metals from Bolivia across the Atlantic to ancient Sumer. Allen has suggested a route from the River Plate, eastward across the Atlantic, past the Cape of Good Hope, via the Indian Ocean to enter the Persian Gulf and Red Sea[49].

In addition to affinity between the symbols found on the Pokotia monolith, Fuente Magna bowl and

---

[47] Thompson, pp.116-117.
[48] Allen, p.101.
[49] Ibid., p.117.

Incan weaving we also find that these symbols are identical to signs engraved on Moche bricks. A common feature of huanca or carved Inca stones are steps cut into the rock [50]. The Inca Throne , an immaculately carved set of shallow steps is similar to Proto-Sumerian signs. Other signs from huacas or carved stones at Rodadero Hill and the White Stone at Chuquipalta relate strikingly to the writing found on the Pokotia and Fuente Magna bowl.

---

[50] Thompson, p.20.

CHAPTER 3: THE DECIPHERMENT OF THE FUENTE MAGNA BOWL

In 1958/60 Don Max Portugal Zamora, a Bolivian archaeologist, learned of the Fuente Magna bowl's existence. Pastor Manjon, Mr. Portugal "baptized" the site with the name it bears today, "Fuente Magna".

The Fuente Magna bowl was found in a rather casual fashion by a country peasant from the ex-hacienda CHUA, property of the Manjon family situated in the surrounding areas of Lake Titicaca about 75/80 km from the city of La Paz. The site where it was found has not been subject to investigation until recently. The piece in question is a little out of place. It is beautifully engraved in chestnut-brown both inside and out. It reveals zoological motifs and anthropomorphic characters within.

Controversy surrounds the writing on the Fuente Magna Bowl. Dr. Alberto Marini, translated the cuneiform writing on the bowl and discovered that these inscriptions were written in the Sumerian writing.

After a careful examination of the Fuente Magna, linear writing I determined that the writing was probably Proto-Sumerian. The Proto-Sumerian writing is found on many artifacts discovered in Mesopotamia. An identical script was used by the Elamites called Proto-Elamite.

Many researchers have been unable to read the writing because they refuse to compare Proto-Elamite and Proto-Sumerian writing with other writing systems used in 3000-2000 BC. I have compared the writing to the Libyco-Berber writing used in the Sahara 5000 years ago. This writing was used by the Proto-Dravidians (of the Indus Valley), Proto-Mande , Proto-Elamites and Proto-Sumerians.

All of these people formerly lived in Middle Africa, until the Sahara began to dry up after 3500 BC. Rawlinson, was sure that the Sumerians had formerly lived in Africa, and he used Semitic and African languages spoken in Ethiopia to decipher the cuneiform writing. Rawlinson called the early dwellers of Mesopotamia: Kushites, because he believed that the ancestors of these people were the Western Kushites of Classical literature.

The Libyco-Berber writing cannot be read using the Berber language, because the Berbers only entered Africa around the time the Vandals conquered much of North Africa. Although the Libyco-Berber writing can not be read using the Berber language it can be read using the Mande language. This results from the fact that the Proto-Mande formerly lived in Libya, until they migrated from this area into the Niger valley of West Africa.

The Vai writing have signs similar to the Libyco-Berber, Indus valley, Linear A of Crete, Proto-Elamite and Proto-Sumerian signs. The Vai people spoke a Mande language.

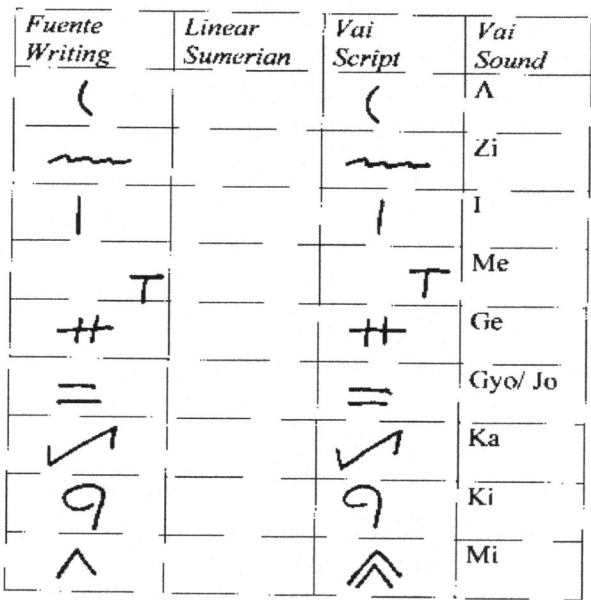

Figure 1: Comparison of Fuente, Proto-Sumerian and Vai Writing

Comparison of Proto-Sumerian and Vai Writing

Fuente Writing	Linear Sumerian	Vai Script	Vai Sound
┐	Dar (to divine)	┐	Ti
✚	Mash (Diviner)	✚	Bi
┳	Me (charms)	┳	Gbe
⊔┬⊔	Gal (great)	⊔⊔⊔ 1. ⊔⊔ 2.	Tu
▽	Du (to make)		Pa
┐		┐	Lu
⟂		⟂	Nia
◢		∣△	Ipa
⊔⌐		⌐⌐	Su

Figure 2:: Comparison of Fuente, Proto-Sumerian and Vai Writing

Using the phonetic values of the Vai script, I have been able to decipher the Indus Valley and Linear A writing.

Given the fact that the Sumerian language is closely related to the Dravidian and Mande languages, and the similarity between the Proto-Sumerian script and the Libyco-Berber and Vai scripts, suggested that I might be able to decipher the Fuente Magna writing by using the phonetic values of the Vai script to transliterate the Fuente Magna writing. Once I transliterated the Fuente Magna signs, I translated the inscription using the Sumerian language.

To test this hypothesis I compared the Fuente Magna writing and symbols from the Vai writing. I found many matches. Next I consulted several works on the Sumerian language and writing system. A couple of these works were C.S. Ball, Chinese and Sumerian (London ,1913), and John A. Halloran, Sumerian Lexicon, http://www.sumerian.org/sumer/ex.htm . Once this was done I was able to decipher the Fuente Magna writing.

The Fuente Magna inscriptions are

written in the Proto-Sumerian script. The Fuente Magna symbols have several Proto-Sumerian signs joined together to represent words and sentences. In figures 1 and 2, I separate the Fuente Magna signs into there constituent parts so they could be interpreted using the phonetic values of the Vai writing. In Figure 4 , I present a copy of the separation of the Fuente Magna signs into their separate parts.

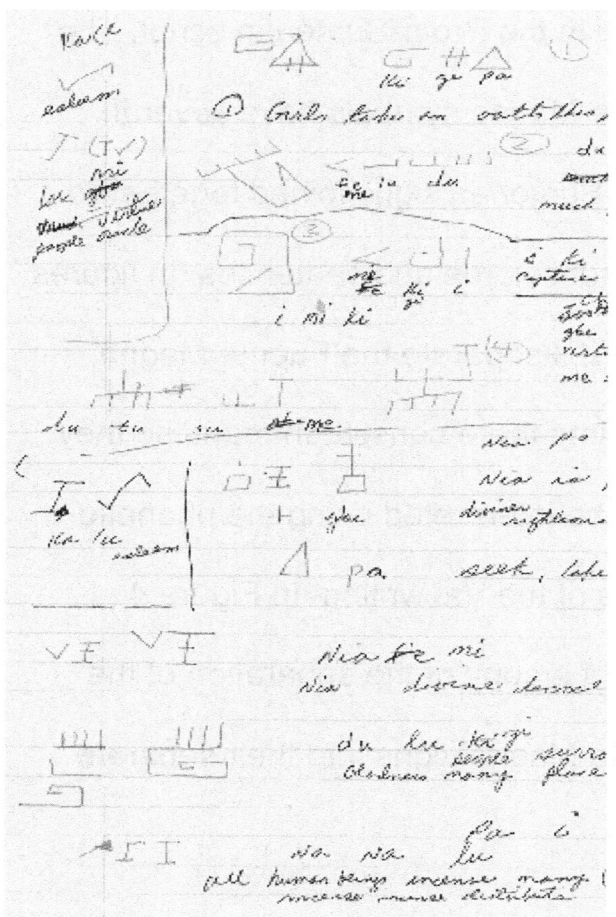

Figure 4: Copy of worksheet used in decipherment of Fuente Magna Writing

Below is a transliteration of the inscriptions on the right side of the bowl. We are reading the inscriptions from top to bottom, right to left.

Transliteration

1. **Pa ge gi**

2. **Mi lu du**

3. **I mi ki**

4. **me su du**

5. **Nia po**

6. **Pa**

7. **Mash**

8. **Nia mi**

9. **Du lu gi**

10. **Ka me lu**

11. **Zi**

12. Nan na pa-I

Below I provide the translation in English

"(1) Girls take an oath to act justly (this) place. (2) (This is) a favorable oracle of the people. (3) Send forth a just divine decree. (4) The charm (this bowl) (is) full of Good. (5) The (Goddess) Nia is pure. (6) Take an oath (to her). (7) The Diviner. (8) The divine decree of Nia (is) , (9) to surround the people with Goodness/Gladness. (10) Value the people's oracle. (11) The soul (to), (12) appear as a witness to the [Good that comes from faith in the Goddess Nia before] all mankind."

Figure 3: The Fuente Magna Bowl

Below is a transliteration of the inscriptions on the left side of the Fuente Magna bowl. As in the earlier inscriptions we are reading the signs from top to bottom, right to left.

Transliteration Left Side Inscription

1. *Tu ki a mash pa*

2a. *Lu me lu ki mi*

2b. *Pa be ge*

3. *Zi*

4. *lu na*

5. *ge*

6. *du po*

7. *I tu po*

8. *lu mi du*

Translation

" (1) Make a libation (this) place for water (seminal fluid???) and seek virtue. (2a) (This is) a great amulet/charm , (2b) (this) place of the people is a phenomenal area of the deity [Nia's] power. (3) The soul (or breath of life). (4) Much incense,

(5) to justly, (6) make the pure libation. (7) Capture the pure libation (/or Appear (here) as a witness to the pure libation). (8) Divine good in this phenomenal proximity of the deity's power."

This decipherment of the Fuente Magna bowl indicates that this bowl was used by the people at Fuente Magna to make libations to the Goddess Nia to request fertility, and offer thanks to the bountiful fauna and flora in the area which made it possible for these Sumerian explorers to support themselves in Bolivia.

It is interesting that the people at Fuente Magna, referred to the Goddess as Nia. Nia, is the Linear A term for Neith. Neith, is the Greek name for the Egyptian Goddess Nt or Neit, Semitic Anat. This goddess was very popular among the ancient people of Libya and other parts of Middle Africa, before these people left the region to settle Mesopotamia, the Indus Valley and Minoan Crete.

This decipherment of the Fuente Bowl (Figure 3) supports the hypothesis of

Awen Dawn that the bowl was used to celebrate the Goddess aspect of the ancient people of Bolivia. The fact that Awen accurately recognized that the figure on the bowl due its Goddess pose : open arms and legs spread, is further support for this decipherment.

Moreover, the identification of symbols on the bowl by Awen, that relate to European signs for the Mother Goddess probably relate to the early influence of Neith on the mainland of Greece and Crete.

The Fuente Magna bowl was probably created by Sumerian people who settle in Bolivia sometime after 2500 BC. The Sumerians had boats that sailed all the way to India-Pakistan. The Sumerians may have made their way around South Africa and entered one of the currents in the area which lead from Africa to South America. These Sumerians were then carried across the Atlantic Ocean by currents to South America (Bolivia).

Ancient Scripts in South America

Cuneiform Writing on the Fuente Bowl

To translate the cuneiform I used Samuel A. B. Mercer's, Assyrian grammar with chrestomuthy and glossary (N.Y.:AMS Press,1966) to compare the signs found on the Fuente bowl with the cuneiform syllabary. To read the Sumerian text I used John L. Hayes, A Manuel of Sumerian: Grammar and text (Malibu,CA:Udena Publications, 2000) and John A Halloran, Sumerian Lexicon, http://www.sumerian.org/sumerlex.htm .

I will translate the Sumerian cuneiform in panels 1 and 2 of the

cuneiform text reading from right to left.

In the first panel there is no mention of Shamash the sun god. This is the Akkadian word for the sun god, the name of the sun god in Sumerian was Utu. Reading the text from right to left top to bottom we find the following;

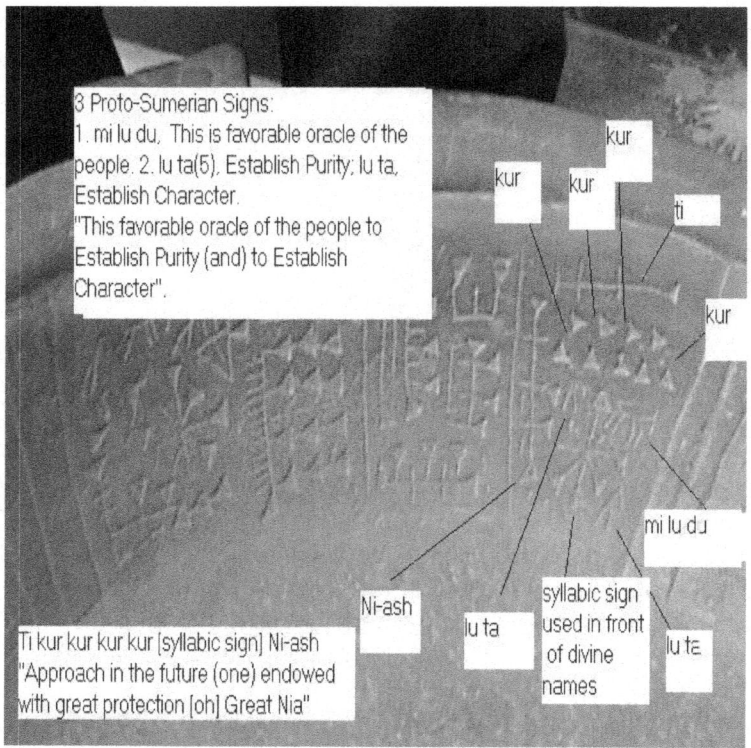

Figure 1: Panel 1

Ti Kur kur kur kur (determinative for divine names) Nia (lit. ni-ash) (Figure 1)

Translation:

"Approach in the future (one) endowed with great protection the great Nia".

"This favorable oracle of the people to establish

purity and to establish character [for all who seek it]".

This first panel is very interesting. There are three Proto-Sumerian signs in this panel. Here we also find the use of the divine determinative. Hayes, page 35 (figure 5a) discusses this sign.

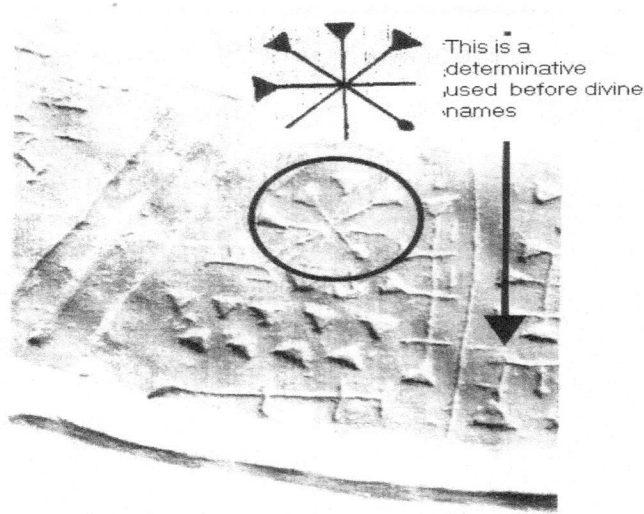

This is a determinative used before divine names

The Sumerian sign used before divine names

I have interpreted the sign Ni-ash as Nia, because of the fact that when a syllable is joined to a consonant vowel form the adjoining sign becomes a single vowel. If we read the signs as Ni-ash it means: "unique awe".

The Sumerian goddess was Nammu, we know very little about this goddess because much of the knowledge about her was lost at the beginning of Ur111. According to Hayes she was recognized as "the mother who gave birth to heaven and earth", the primeval mother, who gave birth to the gods" (Hayes, p.35). This passage suggests that the original name for Nammu was Nia. The quote from Hayes makes it clear that Nammu-Nia was highly regarded and was worshipped as the main god before the rise of any other Sumerian gods.

Ancient Scripts in South America

In the second panel reading from right to left, top to the bottom we find the following:

Figure 2: Panel 2

Transliteration Panel 2:

Pa en ash sa tur

Translation:

"Sprout [oh] diviner the unique advise [at] the temple"

This translation of the first two panels of the cuneiform writing reads as follows:

"Approach in the future (one) endowed with great protection the Great Nia".

"[The Divine One Nia(sh) to] Establish Purity, Establish Gladness, Establish Character"

"[Use this talisman (the Fuente bowl)] to sprout [oh] diviner the unique advise [at] the temple".

Here we have panel 3, of the Fuente bowl. The signs on this panel are very interesting, as in the other panels we see a combination of Proto-Sumerian and cuneiform signs.

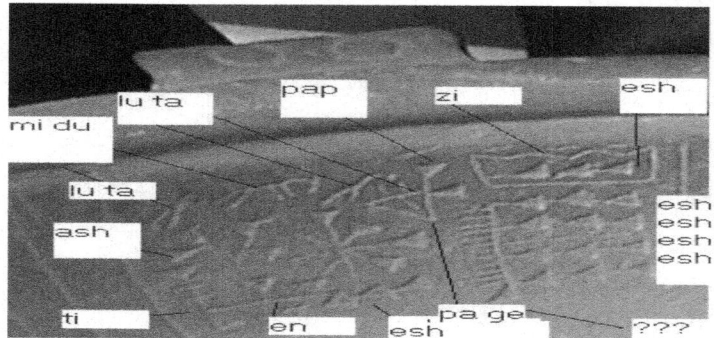

Panel 3

Reading from right to left, top to bottom. We have the following:

Zi esh

The righteous shrine

Esh esh esh esh

Anoint the shrine, anoint the shrine

Pap pa ge

The leader takes an oath [to]

Lu ta mi du lu ta

Establish Purity , a favorable oracle (and) Establish character

Bar nu ash

Open up a unique light [i.e., knowledge, for all]

Ash ti en

Wish for a noble life

The entire panel reads as follows:

"The righteous shrine, anoint (this) shrine, anoint (this) shrine; The leader takes an oath [to] Establish purity, a favorable oracle (and to) Establish character. [Oh leader of the cult] Open up a unique light [for all], [who] wish for a noble life".

Commentary

The cuneiform writing was interesting for two reasons. First, we find that these panels have proto-Sumerian symbols mixed with the cuneiform symbols.

Secondly, whereas, the wedges of most Sumerian cuneiform text point leftward, the wedges of the Fuente cuneiform signs point rightward. This may result from the fact that in the Fuente text, the letters are read from right to left, instead of left to right like the cuneiform text from Mesopotamia.

The passage on the cuneiform panels of the Fuente Bowl seems to be very similar to the Proto-Sumerian inscription on the right side of the bowl. This translation makes it clear that the passage complements my earlier decipherment of the Proto-Sumerian text found on the left side of the Fuente Bowl.

CHAPTER 4: THE POKOTIA MONUMENT

Bernardo Biados sent me photos of a monument he found at Pokotia. The site of Pokotia is around 10 km south of Tiahuanaco (Tiwanaku). These insrcriptions are very interesting because they support the Fuente Magna evidence that the Sumerians formerly lived in South America.

The inscriptions at Pokotia were discovered by Bernardo Biados, Freddy Arce, Javier Escalante, Cesar Calisaya, Leocadio Ticlla, Alberto Vasquez, Alvaro Fernholz, Omar Sadud, Rodrigo Velasco and Paulo Batuani.

Pokotia Monument

This monolith proves that the ancient South Americans had syllabic writing. Zecharia Sitchin, in The Lost Realms (N.Y.: Avon Books, 1990) provides a great discussion of the evidence of writing in ancient Peru and Bolivia (pp. 148-152). He observed that Alexander von Humboldt, in Vues des cordillieres et monuments des peuples indigenes de Amerique (1824) wrote that "It has been recently out in doubt that the Peruvians had besides Quippus , knowledge of a sign script".

It is interesting to note that Sitchin published a picture of skin parchment he claims was formerly in the Peruvian museum at La Paz Bolivia, that have many of the signs found on the Fuente Magna bowl and the Proto-Sumerian script (p.150). According to Sitchin , it was published by Ribero and von Tschudi, in Reisen durch Sudamerika. If this parchment still exist in the museum it will provide even further support for the presence of Sumerian writing in South America.

The area where the Pokotia monument was found is a center of archaeological activity. In this area archaeologist have found numerous sites where pyramidial figures resembling ziggurats. These figures are expertly discussed by M. E. Moseley, The Incas and their ancestors (N.Y.: Thames and Hudson,2000). These ancient sites include Pukara at the northern end of Lake Titicaca, and Chiripa and Wankarani in Bolivia.

The ancient centers of this area are usually made in a u-shape. This style of archetecture was popular in the Huaura and Lurin Valleys. This u-shape tradition at Paraiso date back to 1900 BC (Moseley, p.138). Between 1200-800 BC, copper smelting existed at Wankarani and Chiripa. The Pukara site dates back to 400 BC

The Pokotia inscriptions show affinity to the inscriptions found on the Fuente Magna bowl. Below we list the signs found on the statue from Pokotia.

Ancient Scripts in South America

Pokotia Sign List

	a	e	i	o	u	
	⌣		—		⌢	
			⌢	⋀		**B**
						D
				→		**F**
			≠ ⊥			**G**
					⌐	**L**
	Z		⌐ρ			**K**
	Ɛ	⊥	⋀			**M**
	H					**N**
	△			□ →		**P**
	+ MaSH					
					F S	**S**
	λ O					**T**
					⌢	**Y**
			⌒⌒			**Z**

The Pokotia inscriptions are written in the Sumerian language. The signs are related to the Proto-Sumerian writing. The phonetic values for the signs are the phonetic values of similar signs found in the Vai writing. The sounds for the Vai writing were also used to interpret the Olmec writing and Indus Valley writing.

Pokotia Writing

The Pokotia signs are found on the front of the statue below the hands. The Pokotia signs are found on the right and left thighs of the figure.

The symbols on the Pokotia statue are read from top to bottom, right to left. The signs have syllabic values.

Below are the inscriptions from the left side of the Pokotia stela. These inscriptions are read from top to bottom, and right to left.

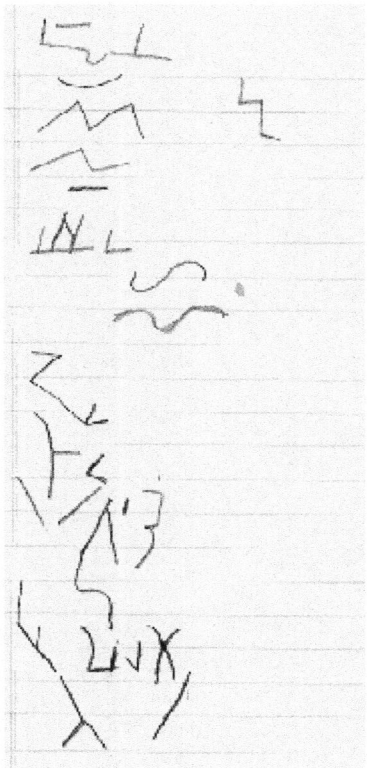

Transcription

Bi

Me be lu

A

Bi

Ka

I

Lu ge me I

Su

U(yu)

Ka mi

Mi I

Me I

Bi I

Mi ka

A I lu ki su

I ta

Translation:

" Distribute/ the opening of the Oracle to mankind./ Proclaim [that Putaki's] offspring (are to) witness esteem./Act justly (now), to send forth the oracle to nourish knowledge./ Appreciate the cult. [All to} witness the divine decree./ Send forth the soothsayer to capture the speech [from the oracle] to make clear the ideal norm [for living, as a guide for mankind]. [Citizens] witness in favor of this human being to create wisdom (for all mankind), and send forth [an example of good] character [Indeed]!"

There is an additional inscription on the left side of the statue. This inscription is listed below:

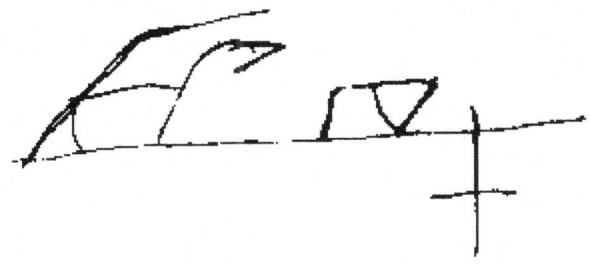

Transliteration:

Mash ge pa po mi lu su ta

Translation

"The Diviner proclaims the phenomenal depth of this area, of the deity's power, to entrust man with wisdom".

On the far right side of the Pokotia statue there are inscriptions which appear to be engraved in a box that provide the name of the oracle. Below is the inscription.

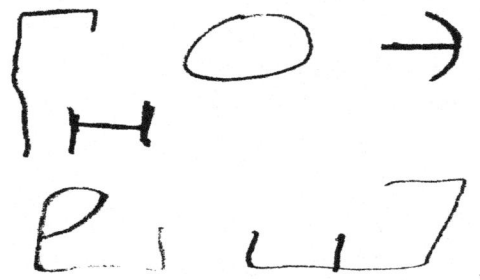

Transliteration

Fo/Pu ta ki

Na

Lu su Lu ki

Translation:

Ancient Scripts in South America

"Good Putaki, a wise man and progenator of (many) people."

There is an additional inscription on the right side of the statue.

This inscription is presented below:

Transliteration

I bi

Ta gu

Mi I

Zi zi

Translation:

" Take an oath to witness character and wisdom. Witness the deity's power [to make for you] a righteous soul".

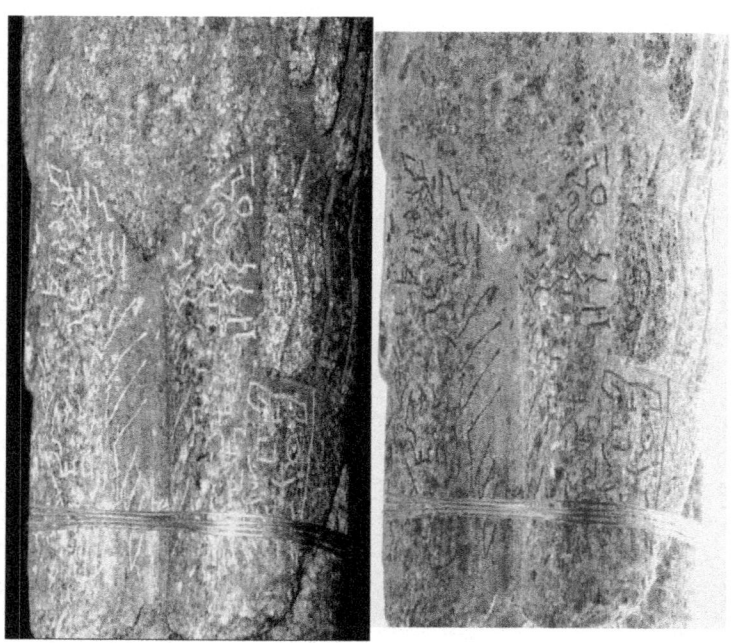

Originally it was believed that there was an inscription written only on the front legs of the monolith, further research indicated that there was also an inscription on the back of the statue and directly below the left hand of the figure.

Inscription on back of Pokotia Monolith

The researchers also found another inscription under the hand of the Pokotia figure.

Inscription under the hand of the Pokotia Monolith

The inscriptions on the Pokotia figure are written in the Sumerian language. The signs used to write the messages on the Pokotia monolith were non-liguture Proto-Sumerian symbols.

Pokotia Sign List

a	e	i	o	ŭ	u	ū
‿			—			ᴗ
	⇄	ᴍ				
				→		→
	≠ ᴵ			=		≣
		•				⌐
ZϚ		⌐ρ				
Ɛ	⊥	∧				
H						
△			▫	→	▫	
+ MasH						
	⋮	⋈			F S	
⋏ O						
					ᴗ	
		ᴡ				

B
D
F
G
L
K
M
N
P
S
T
Y
Z

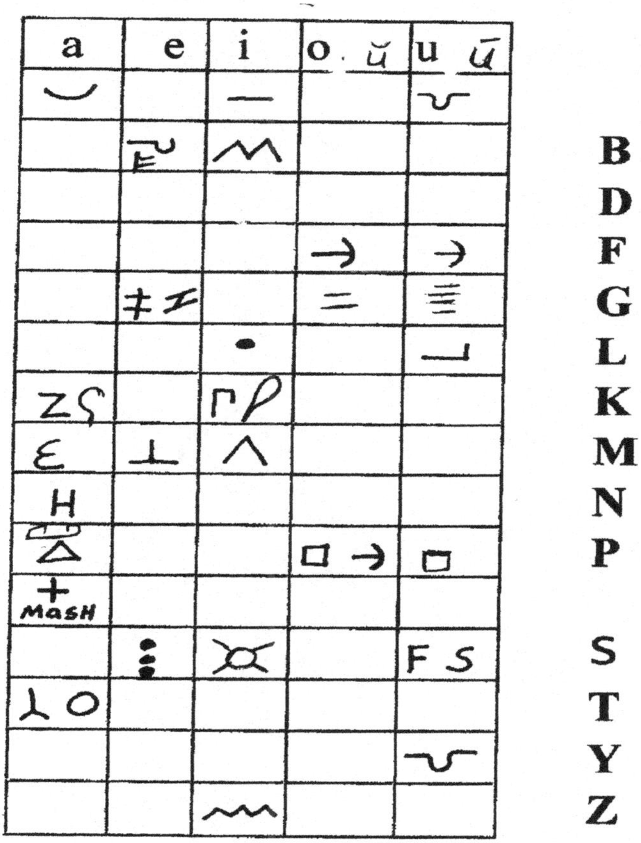

The inscription under the hand on the Pokotia figure is very interesting. It consist of twelve signs.

Transliteration:

Mi

Putaki

Ancient Scripts in South America

Zi

yu u

ka ka mi

i ka be i

Translation

" The oracle Putaki conducts man to truth. (This) esteemed (and) precious oracle to sprout esteem, (now) witness (its) escape".

The Decipherment of the back inscription of Putaki is below. The writing on the back is written in Proto-Sumerian. The language used to read the inscriptions was Sumerian.

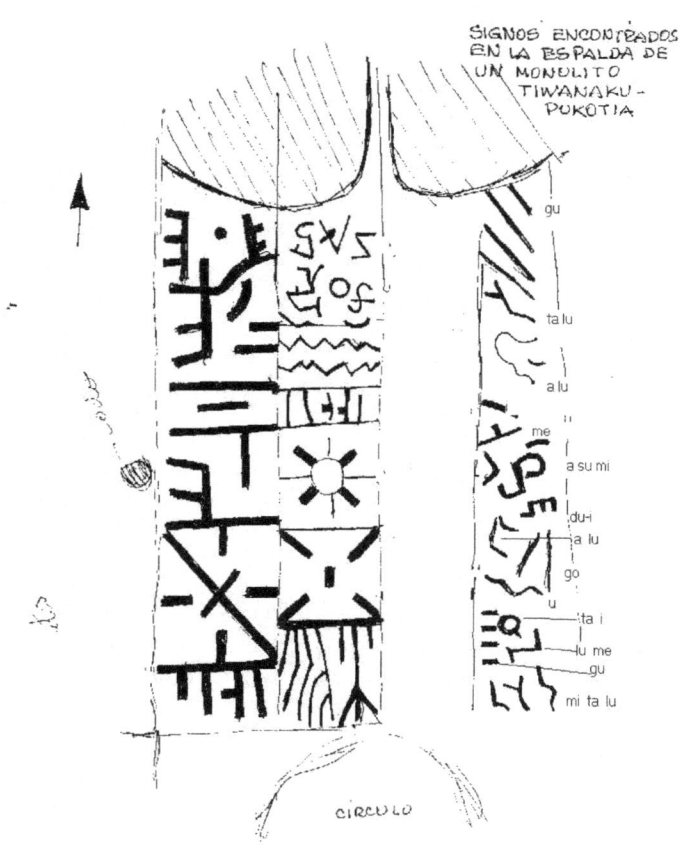

"Proclaim the establishment of character. The strong father (Putaki) to send forth the devination. Strong wisdom (in this) phenomenal area of the deity's power. Capture the speech (of the oracle) . (The oracle is) very strong to benefit (and) nourish the sprouting (of) character. Tell human being(s) (the oracle's) benefit. The oracle to open (up) much (benefit for all)."

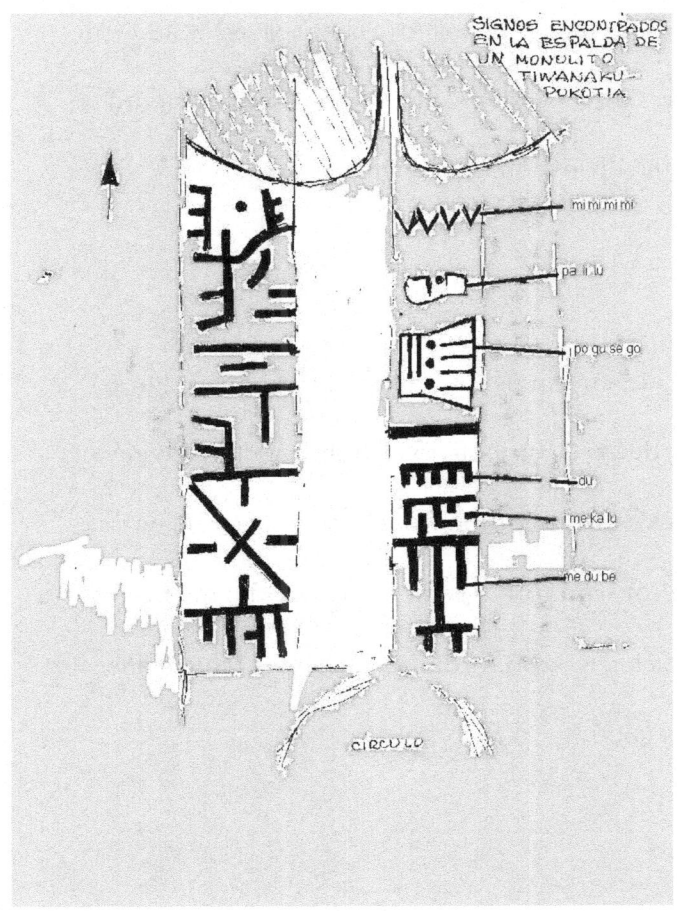

" The ideal norm (is the) oracle (of Putaki). (This) oracle is (in) a phenomenal area of the deity's power". Distribute to all humanity (the divine decree). Snare a portion (of the) pure voice. (The oracle to) send forth gladness. Agitate the mouth (of the oracle), to send forth the divination. The diviner speaks good."

Or

" The ideal norm (is this) oracle. (This) oracle (gives) divine decree. Distribute to all humanity (the divine decree). Snare a portion (of the) pure voice. (The oracle to) send forth gladness. Agitate the mouth (of the oracle), to send forth the divination. The diviner speaks good."

Ancient Scripts in South America

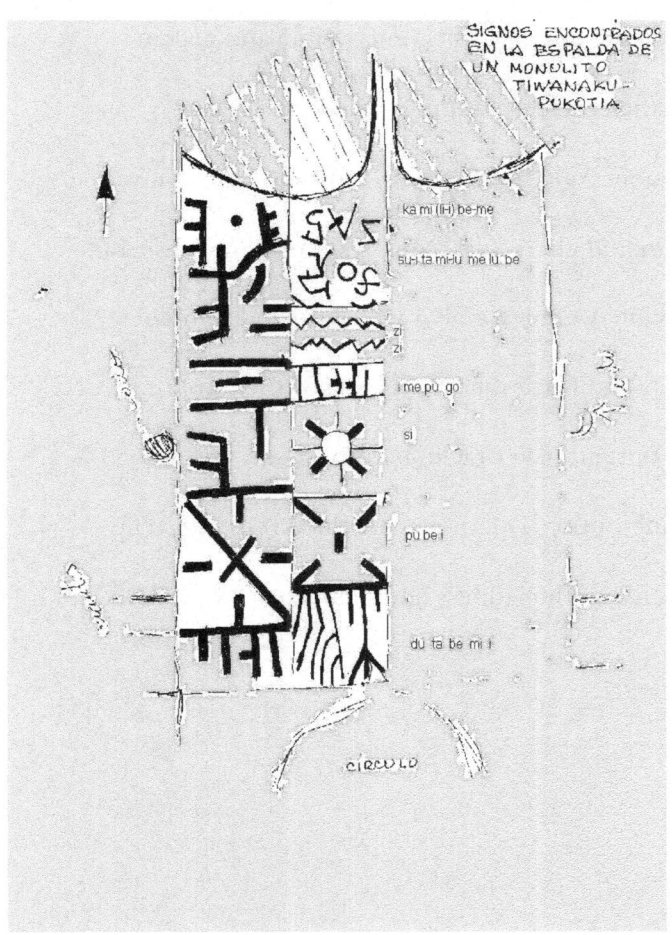

"The divine decree to become visible and glisten (from the oracle's own) mouth. Open up the divination. Agitate the oracle (to) send forth (now) wisdom and character. Open (the oracle) to distribute the divine decree (for all it is) lawful and righteous Good. Send forth the sustenance of the pure oracle. Stand upright (Oh oracle) to appear as a witness speaking purity. The oracle (of Putaki) to open (up and) send forth gladness and character".

Ancient Scripts in South America

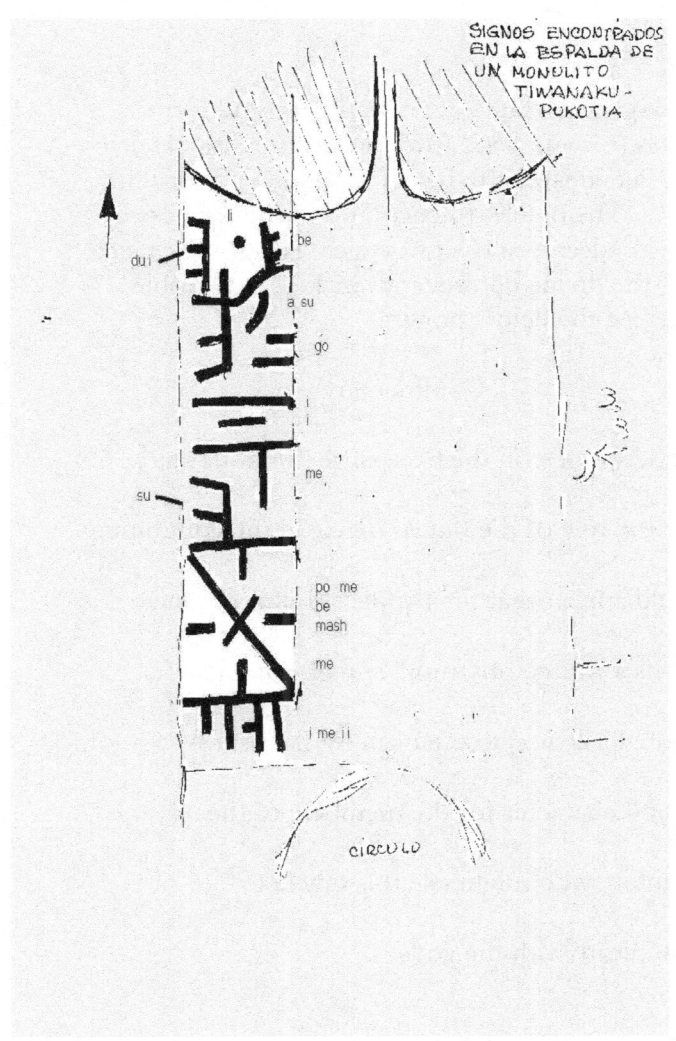

"(Putaki) speaks (in) true measure, to send forth gladness (for all). Send forth nourish(ment). (The oracle Putaki is) the father of wisdom (and) benefit (for all). (The oracle) to become a visible witness of the diving decree and knowledge. (This) pure oracle speaks the divine decree (and) makes (it) a visible witness (of the deity's power)."

Commentary

The inscriptions on the back of the Pokotia statue define the role of the Putaki oracle in the community. It would appear that the people should recognize this oracle as a source of "truth" and glad tidings. Its additional role was to establish rigtheousness, wisdom and good character for the members of the community who might use this oracle to communicate with the gods.

Throughout this inscription the Putaki oracle is called the "father". For example, in column 1, it was written that: "Proclaim the establishment of chracter. The strong father (Putaki) to send forth the divination". And, in column 4, we discover that [Putaki is] the father of wisdom (and) benefit (for all). This suggest that Putaki was recognized as the great ancestor of other oracles in the region.

This suggest that offspring of this oracle was probably situated in other parts of Peru-Bolivia, where the people went to divine the future, communicate with the gods or ancestors, or simply obtain blessing and glad tidings from the oracle.

Discussion

Bernardo's discovery of the Pokotia monument supports the research of the Verrills that the Sumerians came to South America in search of metals. A.H Verrill and R. Verrill, <u>Americas ancient civiliz</u>ations (New York: Putnam, 1953), and J. Bailey <u>Sailing to Paradise</u>, (New York: Simon & Schuster, 1994) maintain that the area around Lake Titicaca may have been called *Lake Manu*, by the Sumerians. According to the Verrills and Bailey the Sumerians came to this area in search of tin. They support this view by a discussion of the Sumerian traditions, that Sumerians set sail to the land west of the Mediterranean that they called the "*Tin land of the West*" or "*Sunset Land*". It is interesting to note that a major center in this area is Potosi. Bailey suggest that Potosi may relate to the Sumerian term *Patesi* the Sumerian term for 'priest king'.

The writing on the Pokotia monument makes it clear that the Pokotia oracle was a heard by many people in ancient Bolivia. This is interesting because the Pachacamac oracle was very popular in this area in historic times. According to Moseley , satellite shrines of one or another of his offspring were worshipped by South Americans (p.68).

During Inca (Sumerian: *En-ka* "Great Lord") times, the temple city of Pachacamac , contained the idol of Pachacamac which was a commanding oracle drawing devotees from Ecuador in the North through Bolivia in the South. People came from far and wide for a

Pachacamac prophesy (Moseley, p.68). The Pokotia statue makes it clear that the popularity of oracles in this part of South America existed all the way back in time to the creation of the ***Putaki oracle***.

There is other support of the early presence of writing in South America dating back to ancient times. Moseley published a number of inscribed Moche bricks and a Tiwanaku portrait head. The characters on the bricks and statue are identical to the Pokotia writing. The symbols on the inscribed Moche bricks are identical to the ***na, I, a, mash/bi, mi, ma, po, ki, ta*** and ***su*** signs listed on the Pokotia sign list above. The symbols on the Tiwanaku head are identical to the ***me*** and ***mash/b***i signs found on the Pokotia statue.

In addition to evidence from South American popular culture (oracle worship) and archaeology there is linguistic evidence that support the Sumerian presence in Bolivia. Mario Montano has found startling linguistic evidence that indicates a Sumerian substratum in the Aymara and Quechua languages. These languages are spoken in Peru-Bolivia.

Diagrama 4   Vocabulario comparativo Sumerio - Aymara - Kichua

Español	Sumerio	Aymara	Kichua
1. Serpiente dios de ancestros	Amaru		Amaru
2. Llama (animal) Dama, alpaca	a-ruru		lulu-luru
3. Camélido (lana suave) canelita	zipu-alpa	allpaqnu	alpaka
4. Dios, Creador Señor, padre	adad	tatakhacol	tata
5. boca	ka	l'laka	
6. Señora, madre diosa madre	mama	mama	mama
7. Ciudad cabeza rey, gobernante	malka	mallku	
8. País de la luz luz	khana	khana	
9. divinidad inger- nal, fuego-lobo	unazu	niña	niña
10. Deíctico, acusativo objeto del	-na-		-na
11. El ave Murasu, totémico	tutu	Tutu	
12. Divino ac. Supremo regenos, formativo	zamama	bama	bama, ba-mama
13. sangre, anal	shirrusu	asiru	
15. Oro, deli	-ki		-ki
16. Montaña Cadena ontológica	kor	kuru	
17. Ñino, e. hijo de ac. Niña, del	titi		titi
18. Sacerdoticio sacer sote, munachera	lukur-	lukur(-mali)	
19. Dios creador	shamash	kamakita-	Kamachiy
20. Iluminación, superlativo purou	n̂ā		n̂ā
luminoso	Iña	Iña	Iña

A principios del cuarto milenio antes de Cristo, aproximadamente, se instalaban en el sur de Mesopotamia los sumerios, pueblo al parecer migratorio de la región nor asiática, región de los pueblos turco-altaicos, con quienes muchos autores los han asociado como idioma y como cultura.

Sin duda los inventores de la escritura, como suele llamárselos hoy en día, se desarrollaron en ciudades como Kix, Lagash, Eridu, Warka (cabe añadir que en Bolivia, provincia Camacho del departamento de La Paz, pueblo de Moqo-Moqo se hallan asentados los aymaras que se reconocen como warkas (de Sumeria?). En verdad estan notable coincidencia que llama a reflexión con respecto a las relaciones lingüísticas que de manera resumida se presentan en el corto vocabulario y el resto para ilustración.

Sin duda ha de discutirse mucho el tema dada las circunstancias que no son los únicos vocablos reveladores de una relación idiomática como que se comprueba.

Se está en condiciones de ampliar respecto a la parte semántica cuya estrecha concordancia no deja otra opción que aceptar lejanas raíces en esta notable cultura del oriente anterior.

Ha de recordarse a don Pablo Patrón, cuyo nombre

As you can see from the above table many Aymara terms relate to the metaphysical world. This is not surprising given this decipherment of the Pokotia statue and the Magna Fuente bowl which indicated that the Sumerians had established many aspects of their religion in Bolivia. There are other Sumerian terms which relate to Aymara. These signs are listed below: It is clear from the above there is regular phonemic correspondence between many of the Sumerian and Aymara.

The linguistic evidence supports the view that many of these Sumerians were miners. The Sumerian term for copper was **urudu**, this term agrees with the Aymara terms for gold *'ouri'* and copper *'**anta, yawri**'*. The similarity between **urudu** and, **yawri** and **ouri** suggest that the Sumerians may have been the first people in the area to exploit the metals found throughout the Titicaca area and Bolivia.

The presence of Sumerian terms in the Aymara language, and Sumerian writing on the Fuente Magna bowl and Pokotia statue make it obvious that Sumerian civilization was formerly widespread in South America.

This leads me to believe that Bolivia and Peru, may represent the "Tin Land of the West" mentioned in the Sumerian inscriptions. If this is ture ancient Bolivia-Peru may have been called the mountains of Sunset or the "Sunset Land", by the ancient Sumerians.

Conclusion

In summary, the Pokotia statue is an oracle. The name of this oracle was Putaki. It would appear that formerly the area where the Pokotia monolithic was found was recognized as a major religious center where citizens came to hear the oracle recited by soothsayers or shamen. The Pokotia area along with other areas further north was probably the Sunset Land.

It is interesting to note that the name for the oracle Putaki is very close to the name of the site (Pokotia) where the artifact was found. This suggest continuity between the name of the oracle and the contemporary place name.

It is interesting to note that the Pokotia statue and Tiahuanaco monuments share similar headdresses and rib impressions along the chest area of several monuments.

I can not provide a date for the Pokotia statue. But the fact that the inscriptions on the Pokotia monument was written in Sumerian, like the Fuente Magna bowl suggest that the Sumerian language continued to be spoken in this area for an extended period of time . This explains why we find Sumerian and Aymara cognate terms.

Ancient Scripts in South America

Pokotia   **Tiahuanaco**

Here we see a comparison of the Pokotia and Tiahuanaco monolithic figures. The figures appear to be either in a setting pose or standing. In both cases the hands are placed on the side of the figures. The hands on the seated figure are placed on the knees.

These statues appear to have the same headdress and similar scarification across the chest or rib cage area. The general situation of similar "scarification" across the chest and headdress suggest that these artifacts may date back to the same period.

Statue from Tiahuanaco

CHAPTER 5: INCA WRITING

The Inca were not illiterate. Many researchers assume that the Inca did not have writing but this is false.

The idea that the Inca and earlier peoples of Bolivia-Peru had writing and centers of learning, is not new[51]. Incan traditions make it clear that they had long possessed both writing and learning centers, centuries before the Spanish settled the area[52]. Our knowledge about Inca writing comes from the historian Fernando Montesinos, who

---

[51] Roberto MacLean y Estenos, Sociologica educacional en el abtiguo Peru . Mexico: Biblioteca de ensayos sociologicos instituto de investigaciones socials universidad nacional , 1955.
[52] David H. Childress (Ed.), Far Out Adventures, Kempton, Ill.: Adventures Unlimited Press, 2001.

visited Peru from 1629-1642. Montesinos traveled around Peru for fifteen years collecting material for his work <u>Memorias Antiguas Historiales del Peru</u> [53] . He recorded many Incan traditions that acknowledged the presence of writing and educational institutions among the Inca[54]. In regards to Andean education, Montesinos wrote that:

> "He *[Torca Apu Capac, the fortieth king of ancient Peru]* founded in Cuzco a University , which was celebrated among them because of their small learning. And in time, according to what the Indians say, there were letters and characters upon parchment and on the leaves of trees, until all this was lost for a period of four hundred years"[55].

Although the Spanish observers called the Incan centers

---

[53] . Fernando Montesinos, <u>Memorias antiguas historialas del Peru</u>, trans. By Phillip Ainsworth. London: Hakluyt Society, 1920.

[54] Steven J. Crum, College before Columbus: Mayans, Aztecs and Incas offered advanced education long before the arrival of Europeans. <u>Tribal College Journal of American Indian Higher Education</u> , 7 (2), (10/31/1991) pp.14-25; and John Collier, <u>The Indians of the Americas</u> (New York,W.W. Norton and Company, Inc., 1947), p.56.

[55] Montesinos, p.53.

Ancient Scripts in South America

of learning universities, Roberto MacLean y Estenos noted that " nothing gives us the authority to talk about the existence of a university in the Incan Empire, although there did exist centers of a select culture (education) destined to the imperial aristocracy. They were called the Yachuhuasi"[56]. I disagree, if the Spanish observers of these institutions called them universities, the Yachahuasi, were in fact universities, no matter what modern writers might say.

The Incan colleges existed up to the time Hernando Pizarro entered Cuzco . The historian Germán Arcineigas wrote that in 1533, Pizarro saw "the monumental Quechua [Incan] university " [57].

---

[56] MacLean y Estenos, p.80.
[57] Germán Arciniegas, Latin America: A cultural history, trans. By Joan MacLean (New York; Alfred A. Knopf, 1967), p.9.

This university may be the Yachahuasi, which was used to train noblemen and administrators for the Incan state. This University was founded by Sinchi Roca at Cuzco[58]. The university was expanded by the ninth Incan king, Pachacutec[59]. Antonio Vazquez de Espinosa, a chronicler of the 1620's, noted that: " To clearly follow with the description of this city of Incas (cuzco) we have to come back to the Huacapunca neighborhood, also called the sanctuary's door, that was located north of the central part of the city. On the south side of that park there was a university founded by king Inca Roca. That university was actually a group of school buildings called the 'schools' neighborhood and known as Yacha Huaci. This was the home of wisemen known as Amautas and poets that would teach science to the students"[60].

The Chronicler Montesinos mentions the tradition of writing among the Inca. This writing was probably taught at the Incan Yachahuaci along with quipus.

D.H. Childress quoting from Hiram Bingham's monumental history of his discovery of Machu Pichu in 1911, titled the <u>Lost City of the Incas</u>, provides an

---

[58] Collier, p.56.
[59] Ibid., p.56.
[60] Daniel Valcarcel, Historia de la educacion incaica (Lima: Editorial Lima, 1960), p. 113.

interesting account of writing among the Incas by Montesinos. Commenting on the rule of Pachacuti VII, Montesinos wrote that "As the people obeyed him with so little certainty, and as they were so greatly corrupted in the matter of religion and customs, he took steps to conquer them, because he said that if those people communicated with his, they would corrupt them with the great vices to which they had given themselves up like ungovernable beasts. Therefore, he tactfully sent messengers in all directions, asking the chiefs to put a stop to superstition and to the adoration of many gods and animals which they adored; and the outcome of this was but a slight mending of their ways and the slaying of the ambassadors. The king dissembled for the time being and made great sacrifices and appeals to ***Illatici Huira Cocha***.One reply was that the cause of the pestilence had been letters and that no one ought to use them nor resuscitate them for, from their employment great harm would come. Therefore Tupac Cauri commanded by law, that under the pain of death, no one should traffic in **_quilcas,_** which were the parchments and leaves of trees on which they used to write, nor should there be any use of letters. They observed this oracular command with so much care that after this loss the Peruvians never used letters and because in later times a learned **_amautu_** invented some characters, they burnt him alive , and from this time forth, they used threads and quipus"[61].

Although this tradition said that the Inca were not allowed to use writing by Pachacuti very interesting. This is interesting because many ancient Incan **_mantas_** or weavings show characters identical to the writing found on the Fuente Magna and Pokotia statute. Many of these

---

[61] Childress, p.438.

manta with writing were published by Felipe Guaman Poma de Ayala's <u>Nueva coronica y buen gobierno</u> of Peru. The provides many interesting facts about the governance, cultural history and religion of the Inca. It has many drawings of Incan dignitaries whose clothing show numerous symbols that relate to the writing found on Fuente Magna and the Pokotia monolith.

There is an Incan tradition that manta were used to record history. Hugh Thompson, in <u>The White Rock: An exploration of the Inca heartland</u>, discussed the textile that recorded the "history of Tupac Amaru", the last Emperor of the Incas[62]. Thompson called these textiles "oral histories" of the Incas[63]. Thompson wrote that: "It is these weavings that much of the oral history of the Andes has found its promptings, along with the quipus, the knotted

---

[62] Thompson, p.274.
[63] Ibid., p.275

cords. This was perhaps one reason why cloth was so obsessively valued by the Incas, far more than if it were just for clothing. There are numerous stories of retreating Inca armies burning the cloth in their warehouses...."[64]. Thompson continued "the Spanish never understood the secret messages contained within the mantas, the weavings, just as they never understood the system of the quipus"[65].

The fact that the Spanish never noticed that the Inca used the mantas to record history, may explain why up to now no one noticed that the mantas, also include writing that relate to writing from artifacts found on Bolivian artifacts by Bolivian archaeologists.

William Burns Glynn, in <u>La escritura de los Incas</u>, identified ten symbols on the Incan mantas, that he

---

[64] Ibid., p.274.
[65] Ibid., p.277.

regards as writing[66]. These symbols collected by Glynn are identical to signs found on the Fuente Magna and Pokotia statue. These symbols are also analogous to the Proto-Sumerian writing of the people of ancient Sumer. The best example of Incan writing is found in the illustrations by Guaman Poma, in the Nueva corónica y buen gobierno[67]

Much of what we can decipher about the writing system of the ancient Peruvians comes *from Felipe Guaman Poma de Ayala's,* **El primer nueva crónica y buen gobierno** (The First New Chronicle and Good Government). This Peruvian chronicle dates back to 1615. Felipe

---

[66] William B.Glynn, La escritura de los incas. Lima ,Peru: Editorial Los Pinos, 1981.
[67] Felipe Guaman Poma de Ayala, El primer nueva crónica y buen gobierno, 1615.

Guaman Poma de Ayala, was a Native American. The Incan writing is found on the robes or *mantas* of the Incan Kings.

Illustration of Inca King from El primer nueva crónica y buen gobierno

The best examples of the syllabic writing of the Inca are Felipe Guaman Poma de Ayala illustrations of the robes of IAVAR VACAC INGA and OTABO INGA .

Ancient Scripts in South America

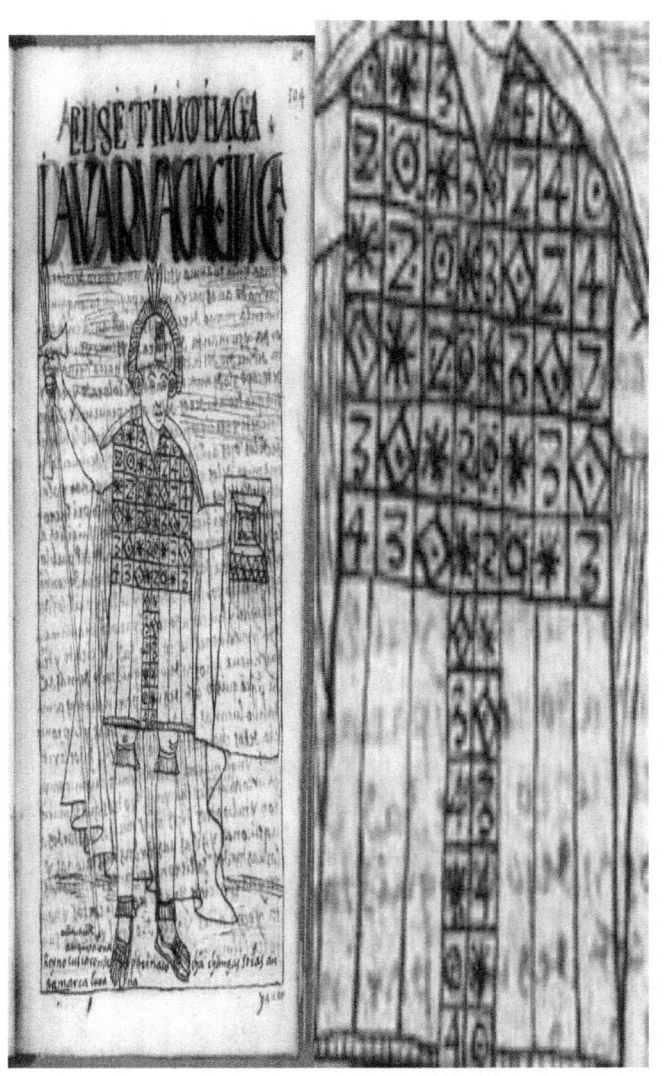

IAVAR VACAC INGA

CLYDE WINTERS

Fuente Magna and Iavar Vacac Inka signs

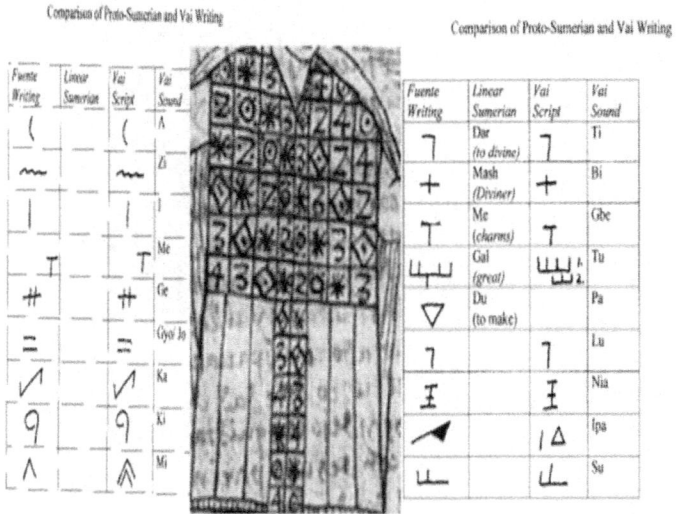

The Inca probably learned Sumerian in their Universities. It appears that the symbols on the mentas of the Inca royals are Sumerian linear signs. As a result, we can read the inscriptions on the mentas.

The Inscriptions on the mentas are usually talismanic messages. The Inca messages are read from right to left.

The transliteration of the Iavar Vacac Inka signs is "Ma an li li ta li li ka an pu li ma gal"; the translation is as follows: " Bound to the Deity, shine and make clear (its) character; send forth glistened esteem the perfect Deity binds greatness. "

Otabo INGA

The Otabo Inga inscription also agrees with the Sumerian writing on the Pokotia monument and Fuente Magna Bowl.

Otabo Signs and Linear Sumerian

The signs on the Otabo Inga Robe are very similar to Sumerian linear signs. These Sumerian linear signs are from C.J. Ball (<u>Chinese and Sumerian</u>, 1913) that was published under the auspices of Oxford University.

Using Sumerian we can read the symbols on

the Otabo menta.

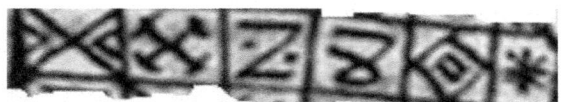

Each symbol in the squares on Otabo's menta , is a CV word . Reading the inscriptions from right to left we *"An pu lu ki ka mash mi mi"*, the translation in Sumerian is " The Deity's perfect man progenitor of (many) people make clean esteem and send forth the Shaman's phenomenal power".

There are three lines of Inca writing on the robe of Roca Inga . In relation to the robe of CINCHE ROCA INGA, from Felipe Guaman Poma de Ayala, **in El primer nueva crónica y buen gobierno,** wrote " and in the middle three betas Tocapo [cloth woven work]". It appears that the writing on Roca Inga's menta, was called "betas Tocapo".

We will read the Inca symbols on the third line of writing from right to left. The transliteration of the signs is " ***Su i ta I An pu-si su I pa i*** ", it reads " Knowledge sprouts Character to send forth to the Shaman , the pure patron's wisdom to sprout (on) the leader—send it forth. "

While on the subject of Peru, an interesting correlation is found in the Women's Encyclopedia (p. 696). Sumero-Babylonian "***mashu***" means "Twin Peaks" [in the sense of 'breasts'] this is similar to Macchu Picchu of the Peruvian Incas. In addition, Mashu and macchu both meant "Mama."

The name for Inca, corresponds to Sumerian: En-ka - Enki - "Great Lord". In addition, Inka and Sumerian/Hebrews share the same decimal counting system; and the Inca *quipu/yupana* cord system is identical to the Sumerian *ephod* 'cord communication system'.

CHAPTER 6: THE AXUMITE PRESENCE IN EARLY AMERICA

There are many Semitic speaking people in the Western Hemisphere today. Although we believe that this is the first time that Semitic speaking people have been here in great numbers, it would appear that during the Arwe and Axumite periods Semitic speaking people established trading colonies in South America, and influenced later South American civilizations.

The Axumite civilization was situated in modern day Ethiopia. The founders of this great African civilization spoke Ge'ez.

Beginning around 200 B.C., Ge'ez speakers began to settle parts of Ethiopia. By 100 B.C., the Ge'ez became the most dominant political group in Ethiopia.

The Ge'ez called the people in the empire **Habesha**. The Kingdom was called **Habeshat**. It was from this term that we get the name **Abyssinia**. Most ancient people referred to the empire as Axum, because of the capital city of the empire. The kings of Axum were titled **negusha nagast** "King of kings".

In A.D. 50, under a new line of Ge'ez kings, Axum was rebuilt east of the original capital at Dar'o Addit Kilte..

The Axumites traded with India. They also controlled all the key harbors on both sides of the Red Sea. The Ge'ez retook Adulis, and expanded their influence in the interior and across the Red Sea in Yemen. By the 2nd century A.D., Abyssinians were cutting off Meroitic trade routes to the Red Sea, and increased their influence in Arabia. For example, after King Afilas of Axum assumed power he held the title "King of Axum, Himyar,Saba, Raydan and Salhen ". This further confirms the political sway of Axum in southern Arabia. The Ge'ez controlled much of Arabia until the 3rd century A.D.

The greatest king of Abyssinia was Aezana/ Ezana who conquered Meroe/Kush and much of South Arabia. Ezana, also helped established Christianity in Abyssinia. Ezana controlled extensive territories in South Arabia, of Himyar, Raidan, Saba

and Sahlen, as well as Siyame to the South of Axum.

The Abyssinians had a large fleet of papyrus ships in the 5th and 6th centuries A.D. The fleet based at Adulis was large and strong. The Abyssinian navy consisted of sewn ships rather than ships made of nails. Procopius, writing at the beginning

of 6th century noted that the Ethiopian ships "they are not greased with pitch or anything else; the boards are not knocked together by iron nails but they are tied with ropes". During this period the Abyssinians were still trading in Iran.

As Abyssinia declined the city-states of southern Arabia became more autonomous. In the 6th century A.D., King Khaleb or Ella Atsbeha became the ruler of Abyssinia. He is recognized as a national culture hero. King Kaleb is famous because he invaded Yemen and put down a rebellion of the Yemenite tribes. He was successful and reestablished Axumite rule in Arabia for a short period of time under a system of indirect rule.

After a period of indirect rule in Arabia, Abyssinian troops established an independent kingdom in Yemen in the 6th century. This kingdom was subjugated by the Persians in the 7th century A.D.

In Africa the Ethiopian Christians were increasingly being isolated by the Muslims. As Islam spread in northeast Africa Abyssinian influence declined except in the mountainous areas away from the coastal ports which had led to the rise of first Punt and succeeding trading powers from northeast Africa for over 3000 years.

There are many correlates between Ethiopia and early Ecuador and Peru. For example, African and South Amerindian weavers used similar looms. In both these areas the weavers used the horizontal loom staked out on the ground, along with the vertical-frame loom with two warp beams. Von Hagen noted that looms"...used by the ancient Peruvians are identical with those of other civilizations with which they had [allegedly] absolutely no contact. A form of back string loom was used in Egypt, a horizontal loom appears in predynastic Egypt, and the one pictured on the tomb Khnemholep (at Beni Hasan) circa 1900 B.C., is identical with those of the Andean and coastal Peruvians".[68]

The Semitic speaking explorers in the Americas who landed in Peru-Ecuador probably reached here originally by accident. Yet the considerable number of Blacks with beards depicted on Mochica art, show there were many of these Axumites living among the Mochicas.

---

[68].Victor von Hagen, Realms of the Incas , (1961)pp.245-46.

Ancient Scripts in South America

The Chinese records make it clear that Axumites made many long voyages in the Pacific and Indian oceans.[69] These

---

[69].Clyde A. Winters,"The Actual dates of the arrival of two Giraffes from Malindi--as gifts--to the Chinese Court of Yung Lo", Asian Profile , vol.3 , no.5 (1975), pp.549-554.

sailors made these voyages in mid-ocean, not coasting near the shore.

We can hypothesize that a group of Ethiopian merchants probably on a voyage to China, Sri Lanka or Malaysia; or on a military campaign to put down a rebellion in one of their Indian Ocean colonies, were captured by the Equatorial Counter Current in their papyrus boats and carried to Peru-Ecuador.

The Axumites probably landed in sparsely populated areas in Peru-Ecuador. In these areas they would have met little resistance from the local Amerindian groups who saw the Semites as giants because of their great height. The experience of the Axumites in building underground dwellings made it possible for them to construct safe

Ancient Scripts in South America

habitation complexes and later step pyramids to bury their elites. The Axumites also probably introduced the building of papyrus boats in South America.

Reed boats may have been first introduced to the Moche by the Axumites. The Mochicas seldom failed to include seagoing reed boat scenes on their ceramics.

At Lake Titicaca, high in the Andes, there are numerous monoliths made in human form and reed boats. These same boats were used as far as California when the Spanish arrived.

There are other possible Axumites influences in South America. The Axumites used the battle club in war. As a result

, Axumite doctors became skilled in trepanning, or true cranial surgery, without killing the patient. This operation was unknown to Europeans until after Columbus discovered

America, yet it was known to the Peruvians. The Axumites and Moche used false heads on mummies.

The ancient Peruvians manufactured bricks of sun-dried clay mixed with straw using the same formula of the Egyptians and Ethiopians. It is also interesting to note that the Peruvian adobes were made in rectangular molds just like in modern Ethiopia.

In South America an ethnic group called Quechua speak a language which is analogous to languages spoken in the Pacific and India.[70] The Quechua Amerindians have an oral tradition which may record the entrance of the Axumites in ships made of reeds or "rushes" that landed on the Pacific

---

[70]. C. Berlitz, <u>Mysteries From Forgotten World</u>, (New York:Dell Publishing Co. 1972) pp.185-86.

coast, off point Santa Elena, close to Puerto Viejo, in extremely remote times. [71] They said that "we had the tradition from our parents"[72].

In 1545 A.D., this oral tradition was recorded by Don Cieza, a Spanish soldier-priest he wrote: "These giants from the sea were so great in statue that from the knee down, they were as tall as an average man. It was amazing to see how the hair hung from their great heads to their shoulders. Yet they were beardless. They ate [probably meant they fight] more than fifty ordinary men. Their eyes were big as plates [**como pequenos platos**]. Their arms and legs were proportionately huge. Some were clad in skins of animals; others quite naked. No women came with them. Going inland they

---

[71].Harold T. Wilkins,<u>Mysteries of Ancient South America</u>, (Secaucus,N.J.:Citadel Press.1974) p.191.

[72] Ibid., p.191.

ravaged the country and finding no water, these builders in great stone set to and sank an immensely deep well in the living rock....and today [1545] the water of this ancient well is so clear and cold and wholesome that it is a pleasure to drink. [This well, made by the giants, was lined with masonry, from top to bottom.] And so well are these wells made that they will last for ages".[73]

Wilkins believes that these giants helped build Tiahuanacu. Commenting on the inhabitants of this ancient South American city he noted that:

> "They were a reddish-skinned race, though among them, as remarkable statuary, dug up from ruins shows, were also black men, with prognathic features. One splendid piece of terra cotta depicts in beautiful colors a high priest of the sun, with remarkably Egyptian eyes and having on his fine, large forehead a mitre and the sign of evolution, called by Bolivian archaeologists, **el simbolo escalonado** (the

---

[73]. Ibid., p.191.

Ancient Scripts in South America

stairway sign)."[74]

This story gives us many details of the culture of these strangers who landed in Peru-Ecuador. First it makes it clear that these colonist-conquerors were taller than the Amerindian; and most importantly it details how they built great monuments out of solid rock. This architectural ability to carve buildings and monuments out of solid rock, was a trademark of the Axumites.

On the Mochica pottery these giants are depicted with black faces. At San Agustin, near the Colombian border we see statues portraying these giants with African features.[75]

Harold T. Williams, in <u>Mysteries of Ancient South</u>

---

[74]. Ibid., p.189.

[75]. Z. Sitchin, <u>The Lost Realms</u> (N.Y. 1990), gives a very good illustration of these statues on page 182, figure 90.

America, says that the ancestors of the Aymara Amerindians were black and lived in underground cities in Brazil. These Aymara Amerindians possessed their own writing system and lived near Lake Titicaca.

THE MOCHICA

There were colonists from Axum living among the Moche of Peru. The Moche empire lasted from A.D. 100-700. The Moche farmed irrigated fields of corn and beans, and raised Llamas and guinea pigs for meat. The Moche or Mochica built pyramids and adobe brick platforms.

A well known characteristic of the Andean people is the absence of heavy beards. Yet many Moche sculptures show images of old men with beards.

The sculptures of the Moche show people of marked racial variations. Some Moche types depicted in Moche art are of Africans Semites, while others reflect the Amerindian types. Dr. Larco Hoyle an expert on the Moche culture, found that many of the skulls of the Moche were of African blacks.[76]

The Moche empire extended over 220 miles along the north Peruvian coast. The Mochicas were warriors, messengers, weavers and doctors. They built roads and organized a courier system which was later adopted by the Incas.

The Mochicas were highly skilled technicians. They made irrigation their greatest concern. In Moche centers we find stone-laid reservoirs supplying the Mochicas with water. In addition they built a gigantic network of canals to bring water into the Mochica settlements to fertilize large stretches of sand.

---

[76]. Larco Hoyle, Los Mochicas . 1939.

The Moche were highly skilled potters. They portrayed their contemporaries with unusual realism and accuracy. Hoyle published many photographs of Mochica works of art that depicted blacks.[77]

For example both the African Semites and South Americans especially the Peruvians, built pyramids to house the dead.[78] The East African Semites also built pyramids.[79]

At Huanca de la Luna, there is a stepped pyramid that was built by the Mochicas. Here we find the walls

---

[77]. Ibid., pp.20-21.

[78]. C.A. Burland, Peoples of the Sun, (New York:Praeger Publishers,1976) p.185.

[79]. A. Heeren, in Historical Researches into the politics...and trade of the Cartaginians, Ethiopians and Egyptians, (vol.1 p.394) wrote that "In Ethiopia and consequently in Meroe, the pyramid architecture was native from the earliest ages."

ornamented with frescos, which show pottery vessels and other objects with the men drawn in attitudes simulating war and defense.

Moche society was militarily organized and there was a rigid system of labor organization. There are many war scenes on Moche pottery which reveal that conflicts occurred between Mochica populations, and non-Mochica who were always shown without clubs.

Due to the Moche use of the club in war, as among the Ethiopians, the Moche had knowledge of brain surgery, undoubtedly to treat severe concussions made by blows to the head by the war clubs. Many trephined skulls show that the Moche patients operated on, usually survived the operation.

Moche doctors also extracted teeth. Skeletal remains discovered in Moche territory indicate that the Mochica doctors replaced missing teeth with false teeth.

The Moche warriors and high personages wore conical helmets similar to the Meroite elites of ancient Kush, with a T-shaped ornament at the apex. The Meroites usually also wore ear and lip ornaments. Ornaments were also placed in the nose.

There may have been some Meroitic people in South America. This view is supported by the style of turban wore by the Mochicas. And the discovery of inscriptions in Ecuador-Peru that are analogous to the Meroitic script.[80]

The Moche men usually wore a turban on their heads or a cap. These turbans agree with the turbans depicted on Meroitic art. The Meroitic frescos show that the warriors

---

[80].D. Diringer, The Alphabet, (New York 1948) vol.2, p.434.

Ancient Scripts in South America

wore multicolored caps with a strip of cloth tied around the cap like a turban. This cloth was left hanging to one side.

There is epigraphic evidence from Ecuador which also supports an Axumite influence in ancient South America. At Cuenca, the Inca capital of Ecuador, the Salesian Father Carlo Crespi collected numerous inscribed artifacts that local Indians claimed came from underground hiding places. Among these artifacts is (1) a gold sheet with a picture of a pyramid, with Ethiopian letters at the foot of the pyramid ; (2) a stone tablet with Ethiopian writing placed linearly below three animals; and (3) a stone pyramid with an elephant and sun symbol at the top of the pyramid and Ethiopian characters placed within the pyramid.[81]

---

[81]. Berlitz, photograph of Cuenca tablets between pages 38 and 39; and Erich von Daniken, <u>In Search of Ancient Gods,</u> New York: G.P. Putnam's Sons 1974) pp.154-155.

Elephants and lions are rarely seen in Egyptian art, but they are common in Meroitic and Axumite art. In Ethiopia the lion was frequently shown on reliefs and sculptures, as well as carved in the rock face on the side of cliffs. Moreover the elephants used in Ptolemaic and Roman times are believed to have been trained by Meorites. And just before the raise of Islam in Arabia, the Axumites attacked Arabia using elephants.

The tablets from Cuenca were written in two writing systems formerly used in ancient Ethiopia. The two stone tablets were written in the Trigrinya language[82], while the inscriptions written on the metal sheet which had figures of a lion, a serpent, a pyramid and elephants with a series of

---

[82]. These tablets are illustrations 203 and 205 in Erich Von
Daniken's, <u>In Search of Ancient Gods</u> , located between pages 38 and 39.

Ancient Scripts in South America

inscriptions along the base were written in Thamudic.[83]

The Ethiopic writing on the Cuenca tablets is in the unvoweled form. This indicates that they date back to the third and fourth centuries A.D. This would correspond to the Moche period.

The Cuenca tablets refer to various aspects of the life of the farmer-soldier (and the traveler). The Ethiopic characters are unvoweled . The same character could be written either right or left , up or down and retain the same meaning. The inscriptions found on the Thamudic tablet are read from right to left.

On Cuenca Tablet 1, the sun figure probably

---

[83].Ibid., illustration 206 and 207. The Thamudic script probably invented during the Punt period in East Africa , served as the model of the Ethiopic and Sabaen scripts.The Thamudic script includes all the signs of these other two scripts.

represented **Zat-Baden** or the Ethiopian sun-god and an elephant we find reference to three things the harp, beer/mead and bread. These three things are associated in Tigrai with the man who is about to make a journey or go to work in the fields.[84]

Cuenca Tablet 1

---

[84]. E. Littman, Publications of the Princeton Expedition to Abyssinia, (Leyden 1910) vol.4, pp.226-233 and pp.197-198.

Ancient Scripts in South America

Reading the tablet from top to bottom we have the following transliteration:

Zat-Baden ,'Ewal , b-g-n z-b-r-k t-b-t.

The Sun God, the Elephant (begana)harp (zebreka)beer (tabeta)bread

The Translation of this inscription is as follows "Zat-Baden (strong as) the elephant. (Give) me the harp, beer\mead and bread".

This inscription may have paid homage to travelers. It is interesting to note that in the modern Ethiopian state of Tigrai, the men usually drink the mead/beer and eat unleavened bread when they go on long journeys for nourishment.

On the other stone tablet from Cuenca we have at the top

of the tablet three animals a bull, an elephant and an ibex (Cuenca Tablet 2)

Cuenca Tablet 2

Under these animals we see a series of Ethiopic inscriptions. Moving from the top of the tablet to the bottom we read : (1) Bull **g-b-t, gebbete** 'to damage, assault; (2) Elephant **y-h-t, yahit** ' to make clear, measure; and (3) Ibex **n-z-t,**

Ancient Scripts in South America

nazezate 'to confess one's sins'.

This tablet probably refers to the warrior creed which may have existed among the Mochica or Huari that once ruled this area. It uses pictograms to denote the role of the soldier.

Because the Ethiopians that settled in Ecuador-Peru were constantly at war with the local Indians, this tablet refers to warfare and probably can be interpreted as follows: "In war it is the bull [**gumah** , of short horns because of his ferocity] that causes damage [to the enemy], and the elephant **('ewal)** that will make the outcome clear,[it is to the] Ibex [symbol of the Mood god] that we must confess our sins [for deliverance]. The presence of these tablets in Ecuador and the depiction of **Sin carved out of hewn rock and mention of the god in Moche traditions all point to the Ethiopian presence in Ecuador-Peru.**

In addition, to **huancas**, there is other support for the early presence of writing in South America dating back to ancient times. Moseley published a number of inscribed Moche bricks and a Tiwanaku portrait head. The characters on the bricks and statue are identical to the Pokotia writing. The symbols on the inscribed Moche bricks[85], are identical to the na, I, a, mash/bi, mi, ma, po, ki, ta and su signs listed on the Pokotia sign list (see Chapter 4) . The symbols on the Tiwanaku head are identical to the *me* and *mash/bi* signs found on the Pokotia statue.

In summary Semites from East Africa probably early settled parts of South America. The Semites of the Moche period may have come from modern Ethiopia

---

[85] M. E. Moseley, The Incas and their ancestors. New York.: Thames and Hudson, 2000.

or Somalia, which served as a major staging area for Meroitic and Axumite navies that took trade goods to nations in the Indian and Pacific oceans[86].

This fact is proven by the discovery of skeletal remains of blacks in Peru and Ecuador.

Although people may have come to South America from Africa, Southeast Asia and the Pacific, Semites from Axum probably greatly influenced the rise of the elaborate monuments made entirely out of stone in Peru and Ecuador and introduced certain types of looms as noted by Victor von Hagen in Realms of the Incas. In addition these blacks played a very important role in the rise of the Mochica empire in Peru-Ecuador.

---

[86] D.A. Phillipson, African Archaeology (New York: Cambridge University Press, 1993) p.172.

CHAPTER 7 : NASCA

Researchers have also found Semitic inscriptions in Nasca. The Nasca culture is characterized by giant geoglyphs in the Nasca valley.

In addition to pictures of animals and geometric designs researchers have found writing. This writing is probably Geez.

William J. Veall, Director Nasca Display Interpretation Project of France sent me inscriptions in the hope I could decipher the writing. This inscription has a total length of 300m, width 25m and the characters are 20 m. The characters were built from small heaps of stones. Each pile forming a character was composed of six/seven piles of stone per character. Reading the signs from left to right we have the following:

Nasca script.

I am not sure that these "geoglyphs" are authentic, because I have not heard of them before. It seems to reason that if they are for real someone would have published them earlier.

Having said this I will still give you my opinion

about the writing. The inscription appears to be a combination of syllabic and alphabetic signs used by several ancient nations in the past.

Some of these signs I can not interpret. If these signs are authentic, they appear to resemble Ethiopic writing. The Ethiopic writing is related to the South Arabia scripts.

To interpret these signs I used Thomas O Lambdin's, Introduction to Classical Ethiopic (Ge'ez) (1978). Reading the text from right to left I believe we might find the following characters:

(1)Hg (<hq) rb z n n. (2) 'w r m s(h)l 's(glottal zed). (3) sg (glottal zed /s/) n n.(4) dn n ys

Transliteration

(1) Carve…increase this move/spread come go down

(2)Water pacify strain

(3)Grace/favor move/spread come

(4)be strong come go out

(1) Come go down (into the earth) and spread this …..

(2) Strain and pacify the water (in the area).

(3) Come and spread (within this region) Grace.

(4) Go out (among the land) and become strong.

The Ethiopic writing has vowel signs attached to each symbol. As a result I can not be sure that my interpretation of the writing is the correct one. To make sure that the translation has some validity I used generic Semitic roots to interpret the signs. These roots can be found in any dictionary of Semitic languages.

Semitic roots

hg (hq), to carve

rb, (increase

z, this

n , to come, to move

'w, go down

Ancient Scripts in South America

m, water

'a (asa), to press, to make, to strain

s(h)l, to quiet, to pacify

sg, (saga), grace, favor

dn, be strong, to adhere

ys, go out

As I said earlier I don't know if these inscriptions are authentic or if someone just put these letters together to deceive us. There appears to be too many /n/s in the inscriptions for my taste.

If they are for real it would appear as if the inscription were written for someone to see from the air. Some people have claimed that the Chimu, may have used balloons to travel. If this is true these inscriptions way relate to this period. They suggest that the signs may have been an invitation to the balloonists viewing the signs to form a settlement in the area.

I am not an expert on Nasca, but it would be interesting if this area was settled in the past, and provided arable land and water for ancient farmers. The archaeological evidence supports the view that the Nascans practiced agriculture. C.A. Burland observed that: " Agriculture was conducted in both areas of the coast with much ceremony. There were planting and harvest festivals. As the coastal region was a grim desert, the river valleys which irrigated narrow areas were precious to the people....In the south around Nasca one finds pictures of plants, and many have depictions of curious beings walking among the crops"[87].

---

[87] Burland, p.178.

CHAPTER 8: THE MALIANS IN SOUTH AMERICA

There were also many Malian inscriptions found in South America. Led by Mansa Abubakari of the Mali Empire of West Africa, thousands of Malians sailed to the Americas[88].

The expeditionary force of Mansa Abubakari, must have been immense, because the average boat on the Niger, in the 1500's A.D., could carry 80 men. This means that anywhere between 25,000 to 80,000 men may have sailed from Mali along with

---

[88] Clyde Winters, African Empires in Ancient America. http://www.amazon.com/African-Empires-Ancient-America-Winters/dp/0615796583

Mansa Abubakari.

The mention of a violent current in mid-ocean by Abubakari's captain may refer to the Atlantic ocean currents which can carry a boat from Africa to the Americas.

We can hypothesize that Abubakari and his expeditionary force probably left the city of Niani, by canoe and traveled down the NIger to the Gulf of Guinea. From here the expeditionary force was probably carried by the Guinea Current out into the Atlantic where it met the South Equatorial Current. The South Equatorial Current carried the Mali explorers to Brazil.

Abubakari's ships would not be the last vessels to be carried to Brazil. For example, in 1500 ,

Alvares Cabral's ship was captured by the North Equatorial Current and swiftly taken to Brazil.

In addition to high boat technology the ancient Manding had their own writing system. The so-called Libyco-Berber inscriptions found throughout the Western Sahara in the Air, Mauritania and Morocco were engraved by the ancient Manding in their own logo-syllabic script. At many Western Sahara and sites in North and South America, we find the Mande totem sign **Kangaba** (the lizard or serpent) engraved.

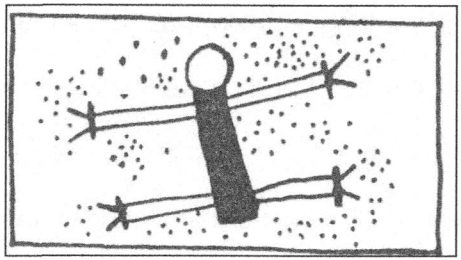

Kangaba Sign

The earliest Proto-Mande inscriptions are located at Oued Mertoutek which has been dated to 3000 BC [89]. The Oued Mertoutek signs are identical to the Vai signs and the Manding signs located in the Grotte de Goundaka in West Africa [90].

---

[89] F.R. Wulsin, The Prehistoric Archaeology of Northwest Africa. Papers of the Peabody Museum of American Anthropology and Ethnology, Vol.41, No.1, 1941.
[90] Leo Wiener, Africa and the Discovery of America, vol.3, (Philadelphia, 1922) pp.269-271; C.A. Winters "The ancient Manding script". In

The Manding writing is analogous to the Indus Valley, Minoan Linear A, and Olmec writing. The Proto-Manding wrote on stone, wood and dried leaves. Ink was made from soot and liana. The Bambara (Manding tribe) claim that they once carved their royal inscriptions/archives on tablets of wood. Today ancient Manding writing systems survive among the Manding secret societies.

Upon arrival in America the Manding sailed along the coast until they found rivers like the Orinoco in Venezuela, and Amazon in Brazil which they used to move into the inland parts of South America. Along these rivers the Manding have left

---

Blacks in Science: Ancient and Modern, (ed.)by Ivan van Sertima, (London: Transaction Books, 1983) pp.208-214.

many inscriptions to point the way to good camp sites for Abubakari and the main expeditionary force[91].

> In Venezuela and Brazil we see the common Manding sign for habitation ⊞ , while in Brazil and elsewhere we find the Manding character for **Nu** 'habitation':
>
> One of the most common signs associated with Anaszi, southern American culture is ⋎ . This same sign painted in red occurs at the Grotte Goundaka, and other sites in Mali (Szumowski, 1955). In the Painted Desert Petrifies Forest National Park, we not only find the above sign, but the **so** sign as well. The word **so** or **su**, in Malinke-Bambara, means habitation among other things.

Many of these inscriptions have been found along

---

[91] M. Hamidullah, Muslim discovery of America before Columbus, <u>Al-Ittihad</u>, vol.4 (no.2) ,(1968) pp.7-9.; and C.A. Winters, "Islam in Early North and South America", <u>Al-Ittihad</u>, vol.14 (no.3-4),(1978)pp.57-67.

the Rio Chao river in the state of Alagos in Brazil . The first evidence of African inscriptions in Brazil were discovered in Bahia around 1753, by Padre Tellesde Menezes, in Marajo[92]. Other inscriptions have been found in the states of Bahia near the rivers Para-oacu and Una that appear to be African.

The Brazilian inscriptions provide diverse messages. Some of these inscriptions were meant to warn the Manding expeditionary force not to camp in certain areas because of health risk or military threat .

---

[92] B.A. Silwa Ramans, <u>Inscripcoes e tradicaes do America Prehistorica</u>, Rio de Janeiro, 1930. 2 volumes,

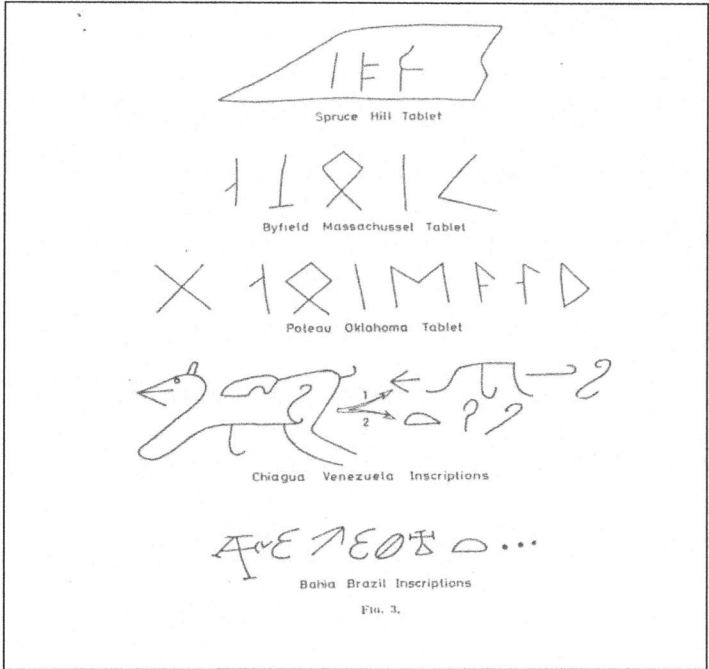

Malian Inscriptions in South America

These inscriptions are of two kinds. One group of inscriptions were meant to warn the Manding expeditionary force not to camp in certain areas. Inscriptions in this category are found at Piraicaba, Brazil. Another group of inscriptions were left in areas suitable for settlement.

Once a safe place was found for settlement, the Manding colonists built stone cities or mound habitations. One of these lost cities was found in

A.D. 1753, by **banderistas** (bandits). These inscriptions were found in the State of Bahia,Brazil by Padre Tellesde Menezes, in Marajo near the

Para-oacu and Una rivers engraved over a mausolea. They tell us that the personage buried in the Tomb was named Pe.

The most startling evidence of Malians in Brazil , is the "Brazil Tablet", discovered by Col. P.H. Fawcett in an unexplored region near the Culuene river. The interesting thing about this Tablet, was the fact it had "African pigment" and features (printed above)⁹³.

Fig. 2. — Brazil tablet discovered by P. H. Fawcett.

---

⁹³ Harold T. Wilkins, <u>Mysteries of Ancient South America</u>, (Secacus, New Jersey:Citadel Press, 1974), pp.40-45; and Branco, p.146..

The personage in this Tablet was an elite of Malian colony in Brazil. Evidence suggesting a Manding origin for the Brazil Tablet are 1) THE CROWN worn by the personage on the tablet; 2) the Manding inscriptions inscribed across the chest and feet of the figure on the Fawcett Tablet; and 3) the evidence of breeches similar to the Manding style military uniform worn by the personage depicted on the Fawcett Tablet.

The decipherment of these inscriptions detail the burial place, and cause of death of a **Mansa** or Mande King. it appears that the Mansa on the Brazil Tablet" was named **Be**. It tells us that **Be**, was buried in a hemisphere tomb (i.e.,mound) [94].

The Malians in South America also built their homes on top of mounds. There major centers of habitation appear to have been Panama and Venezuela in addition to Brazil. In Brazil there are many megalithic structures that seem to have there prototype in Africa. For example, in Alagoas we find many stone monuments similar to those found in West Africa, such as stone circles formed by rocks placed vertically on the ground.

The habitation mounds in Brazil are called **sambuquis**. Some of the **sambuquis**, have radio-carbon dates going back into pre-history, while many of the mounds where artifacts have been

---

[94] C.A. Winters,"The influence of the Mande scripts on American writing systems", pp.429-432.

found are related to the cultures of Venezuela, and have dates contemporaneous with the Malian voyages.

Malian inscriptions have also been found in Uruguay. Using satellite images William J. Veall has found many inscriptions along the Uruguay coast that were written by Malian explorers[95]. The Malians wrote the inscriptions in the Mande or Manding language.

---

[95] WILLIAM JAMES VEALL, Sea-Farers from the Levant: Do Ancient Inscriptions Rewrite History of the Americas? - Part 2 http://www.ancient-origins.net/ancient-places-americas/sea-farers-levant-do-ancient-inscriptions-rewrite-history-americas-part-2-020350#ixzz3r1xXsQOD

Ancient Scripts in South America

Chart of Manding inscriptions and their transliteration

	Characters	Transliteration	Meaning read right to left
1	𐍈:	pe ta yo	dig here the large hemisphere tomb
2	⋯⋀	se fe	advance to the vacant land
3	A ? ⌑	pa po -i ga	very pure hearth
4	⅋ ℟ ⊔	yo ta gbe	give existence this place virtue
5	⋯𐍈 °°	li pe se poka	indeed flat country (of) pure land
6	𝟻 ℟	poka lu	the pure land hold (it) upright
7	𝒥 ∄ 𝒴	gbe yu gbe pa yo	to become a vital white spirit a mark of admiration that is perfect
8	⋯⋅	pe se	prodigious sucesss
9	c 9 ⊃ ϟ	be a ki lu	discover amazing order (and) hold (it) upright
10	⅋ △ ⊃ 𝒴	le a pa su	the surface is amazing flat country (for) a village
11	A : ▽	pa gyu ga	??
12	⋈	po gbe	sanctified
13	˙𐍈˙<	fe se poka	to desire success (on the) pure land

The inscriptions along the Uruguay coast are similar to inscriptions found along rivers in Venezuela and Brazil. They were engraved along the coast to tell the Malian colonist the best places to settle in this part of South America.

FINAL WORD

King Sargon I , of Sumer-Akkad claimed that the Sumerians got their tin from a place called **Kuga-Ki**, the **Western Tin Land** .The wide variety of inscriptions and writing found in South America make it clear that many Old World visitors left a tradition of writing among the South Americans . This view is supported by the Incan tradition of writing in their culture in addition to **quipus.**

The inscriptions discovered by Bernardo Biados and his team proves that the ancient South Americans had syllabic writing. This writing system as proven by the inscriptions on the Pokotia statue, Fuente Magna Bowl and Incan mantas worn by their Kings was Proto-Sumerian.

The Sumerians made it clear that **Kuga-ki** was situated West of Sumer. An Assyrian official scribe in the capital city of Assur, in the 8th century B.C, wrote a tablet detailing the regions under the control of Sargon I. The Sumerologist Prof. Sayce who translated the tablet relates that it said that Sargon's empire *includes "the countries from the rising to the setting of the sun, which Sargon the . . . king conquered with his hand," included amongst many other lands "the Land of Gutium," "the land of the Muru (or*

Amorites)" and "the Tin-land country which lies beyond the Upper Sea (or Mediterranean)[96]."

This tablet makes it clear that Tin-land or Kuga-ki, was **"beyond the Upper Sea (or Mediterranean)"**, or out into the Atlantic Ocean.

Sumerian and Assyrian mariners sailed their ships to Magan (Egypt), Meluhha (Punt or Northeast Africa) and Dilmun (Indus Valley). The fact that Sumerians and Assyrians sailed their ships as far away as India makes it clear that these sailors were more than capable of sailing their merchant ships to Brazil and Peru-Bolivia.

---

[96] Text is published in Keilschrifttexte aus Assur verschiedenen Inhalts 1920, No. 92

Sargon I, ruled Sumer-Akkad between 2800-2750 B.C. But we can be sure that Sumerians had been trading with **Kuga-ki**, prior to this date because the South Americans used the Proto-Sumerian syllabic script to keep their records.

Kuga-Ki
The Western Tin Land
of the Sumerians

Ancient Scripts in South America

The Sumerians probably first made contact with Kuga-ki, via the Atlantic currents that take you from Africa to Brazil. Prospectors probably reached Brazil, and sailed down the Amazon river until they found large tin deposits in Bolivia-Peru. Once they established mining operations in the area, local people probably began to work in the mining operations and adopted many Sumerian customs, linguistic terms and the social technology of writing, i.e., the Proto-Sumerian script. This means that writing has a long tradition among the people of Bolivia-Peru.

Zecharia Sitchin, in <u>The Lost Realms</u>, provides a great discussion of the evidence of writing in ancient Peru and Bolivia [94] He observed that Alexander von Humboldt, in <u>Vues des cordillieres et monuments des peuples indigenes de Amerique</u> , wrote that "It has been recently out in doubt that the Peruvians had besides Quippus , knowledge of a sign script".

It is interesting to note that Sitchin published a picture of skin parchment he claims was formerly in the Peruvian museum at La Paz Bolivia, that have many of the signs found on the Fuente Magna bowl, the mantas of Incan Kings, Pokotia statue and the Proto-Sumerian script . According to Sitchin , it was published by Ribero and von Tschudi, in

Reisen durch Sudamerika. If this parchment still exist in the museum it will provide even further support for the presence of Sumerian writing in South America.

The area where the Pokotia monument was found is a center of archaeological activity. In this area archaeologist have found numerous sites where pyramidal figures resembling ziggurats. These figures are expertly discussed by M. E. Moseley, The Incas and their ancestors . These ancient sites include Pukara at the northern end of Lake Titicaca, and Chiripa and Wankarani in Bolivia.

The ancient centers of this area are usually made in a u-shape. This style of architecture was popular in the Huaura and Lurin Valleys of Peru. This u-shape tradition at Paraiso dates back to 1900 BC. Between 1200-800 BC, copper smelting existed at Wankarani and Chiripa. The Pukara site dates back to 400 BC. Bernardo Biados' discovery of the Pokotia monument supports the research of the A.H Verrill and R. Verrill, Americas ancient civilizations , and J. Bailey Sailing to Paradise, maintain that the area around Lake Titicaca may have been called Lake Manu,by the Sumerians. According to these authors the Sumerians came to this area in search of tin. They support this view by a discussion of the

Sumerian traditions, that Sumerians set sail to the land west of the Mediterranean that they called the **"Tin land of the West"** or **"the Sunset Land"**. it is interesting to note that a major center for mining in Bolivia-Peru is Potosi. Bailey suggest that Potosi may relate to the Sumerian term Patesi the Sumerian term for 'priest king'. There is other support of the early presence of writing in South America dating back to ancient times. Moseley published a number of inscribed Moche bricks and a Tiwanaku *(Tiahuanaco)* portrait head. The characters on the bricks and statue are identical to the Pokotia writing. The symbols on the inscribed Moche bricks are identical to the *na, l, a, mash/bi, mi, ma, pa, ki, to* and *su* signs listed on the Pokotia sign list above. The symbols on the Tiwanaku head are identical to the **me** and **mash/bi** signs found on the Pokotia statue.

In addition to evidence from South American popular culture (oracle worship) and archaeology there is linguistic evidence that support the Sumerian presence in Bolivia. Mario Montano has found startling linguistic evidence that indicates a Sumerian substratum in the Aymara and Quechua languages. These languages are spoken in Peru-Bolivia.

As you can see from the above table many Aymara terms relate to the metaphysical world. This is not surprising given this decipherment of the Pokotia statue and the Magna Fuente bowl which indicated that the Sumerians had established many aspects of their religion in Bolivia.

The linguistic evidence supports the view that many of these Sumerians were miners. The Sumerian term for copper was **urudu**, this term agrees with the Aymara terms for gold **'ouri'** and copper **'anta, yawri'**. The similarity between **urudu** and, **yawri** and **ouri** suggest that the Sumerians may have been the first people in the area to exploit the metals found throughout the Titicaca area and Bolivia.

The presence of Sumerian terms in the Aymara language, and Sumerian writing on the Fuente Magna bowl and Pokotia statue make it obvious that Sumerian civilization was formerly widespread in South America.

This leads me to believe that Bolivia and Peru, may represent ***Kuga-Ki*** mentioned in the Sumerian inscriptions. If this is true ancient Bolivia-Peru may have been called the ***"Sunset Land"***, by the ancient Sumerians.

Ancient Scripts in South America

Made in United States
Orlando, FL
12 April 2022

16784065R00108